EARTH ANGELS

Earth Angels

PORTRAITS FROM CHILDHOOD AND YOUTH

Susan Cahill

Harper & Row, Publishers

New York / Hagerstown / San Francisco / London

FIRST EDITION

ISBN: 0–06–010621–2

LIBRARY OF CONGRESS CATALOG NUMBER: 75–23875

Designed by Sidney Feinberg

76 77 78 79 0 1 2 3 4 5

For Tom

1

How big is Martha?
So-o big!

The bars are big too . . . Down! Out! Run run as fast as you can you can't catch me I'm the gingerbread man . . . Daddy is making a fence for the driveway. But it opens, like the church and the steeple.

> *Here's the church and here's the steeple.*
> *Open it up and see all the people.*

Daddy says that on his big fingers . . .

Our father had to go to Boston because he was building submarines to beat the Germans with. Our mother was gorgeous. Every morning she put on her emerald earrings and went to P.S. 91 to teach schoolchildren. When she stuck in her hatpin the doorbell rang. I got stuck with Mrs. McCann.

> *Here's Mrs. McCann, Mrs. McCann.*
> *No more wet pants, no more wet pants . . .*

She had one hundred grandchildren. Mother said she could toilet-train a horse. When the air-raid sirens blew, Mrs. McCann crawled under the piano and prayed on her rosary beads. I turned on the Hoover. Mother called Mrs. McCann "the salt of the earth."

"*Saw-ger-teez . . . West* Saw-ger-teez . . . up the Hudson River in the Cats-kill mountains." I practiced saying the name of the strange place. Mother put the colander and the egg beater into cartons. We were going to the mountains for Mother's nerves. Nony told Sister Mary Imelda the B-12 shots hadn't worked and now the doctor said the best medicine for Mother would be a summer in the mountains. Sister said, "Now, dearie, you tell your dear mother that my own dear family owns a cottage up in the Catskills and it is for rent!"

We went by boat, on the *Alexander Hamilton.* From the top deck you could see the river going on ahead of us forever, past the cliffs like giants which mother called the Palisades. A man and a woman kissed each other the whole time the whistle blew at Poughkeepsie. Daddy called them real hell-raisers.

Something strange happened when we got to our cottage. A man drove us there by taxi and all along the bumpy road you could see the mountains stretched out on both sides like the black panthers in the zoo. The taxi stopped in front of a white church. From the road we walked across a field. Ahead of us was the forest, not a back yard. As we got to the end of the path, a lot of tiny birds flew out from the porch, singing and flying skiddy circles over our heads. Then they flew up into the sky that was covering every place below with rose color. The birds were called phoebes.

Summer in Saugerties was as good as Christmas. After lunch, while mother took her nap, Irene taught me to float in Paradise Hole. Nony practiced diving off the ledge where Irene said there were snakes. On Friday nights we put on our dimity dresses and went up to the road to wait till Daddy came from the city. The doors of the white church were open and from the road you could see the blue vigil lights waving in front of the Blessed Mother's altar. The church was named "Our Lady of the Mountains."

Daddy always brought a box of Schrafft's fruit sticks for the three of us, *The New York Times* for his "best gal," our mother, and an Ebinger's coffee cake for everybody. We barbecued chicken outside on Saturday nights and when the mosquitoes came and it got dark, everyone sang songs around the piano. Mother's sister, Aunt Isabel, cried when mother played "Lili Marlene" because her husband George was overseas fighting. Irene's favorite song was "The White Cliffs of Dover," Nony knew all the words to "Swinging on a Star," and my favorite was "There were three little sisters, three little sisters. Each one only in her teens. One loved a soldier, one loved a sailor, and one loved a guy from the Marines."

We went to Our Lady of the Mountains for Mass on Sunday mornings. Daddy didn't come with us because he wasn't a Catholic and he had to stay home and fish my shoes out of the hole in the outhouse before he went back to the city. At Mass I lay down on the pew behind Irene and Nony and didn't wake up till it was time to sing. Father Finnegan walked up and down the aisle singing and swinging his arms like a bandleader. When he told the people to pray for the soldiers I said prayers for the Germans and the Japs. When Irene and Nony and I had fights, Daddy said, "Break it up fast, you three. Somebody, give in!" The soldiers had been fighting since before I was born. I tried to understand how you could fight for *years* without giving in once.

It was my fault that Daddy missed most of Irene's graduation from St. Francis Assisi School. The whole time the diplomas were being given out, he and I were hunting all over the parish hall for the Girls' Bathroom. By the time we got back to the church, Irene wasn't a grammar school pupil any more. She was a high school girl.

The church vestibule was full of parents and grandparents and graduates in caps and gowns. Our family was standing near the Baptism room shaking hands with the Principal and Irene's old teachers. Then I saw Irene pushing her way toward us through the crowd. She looked so pretty in her long white robe with the gold satin collar. Her hair had stayed curly, she had on her first pair of high heels, and her pimples had gone away in time for graduation day. She showed me and Nony her diploma, which was tied up in a royal blue ribbon.

But then Sister Dennis Marie, her eighth grade teacher who beat the boys, came up to us. She said "Congratulations" to Irene, but when she went to shake hands with my mother, the fight started. My mother would not shake hands with her. She said in a very bold tone of voice, "No congratulations, please, Sister Dennis Marie. What we expect from you is an apology."

The nun looked as if she might get sick. I knew her nickname was "Dennis the Dukes," but I did not think she'd dare sock my mother.

"Did you or did you not say to your class, Sister, that any girl who went to public high school would lose her *purity?*" When she was trying to get to the bottom of something, my mother always said, "Did you or did you not," but I had never heard that last word before.

"Mark my words, Sister, four years from now, Irene will know more about *purity* than you will ever know about *charity.*"

I didn't know what that one meant either. But "Mark my words" was another one of my mother's favorite expressions.

The Dukes was holding on to the crucifix of the big rosary beads hanging off her belt.

"I only meant that it is a shame a girl as bright as Irene cannot go to a better high school than Bayside, Mrs. Girlinghausen." She pronounced our name wrong. She said "Girling-*ho*-sen" instead of "Girling*how*sen."

I looked up at the nun's sore cheeks and scary eyes and hoped she'd be dead by the time I got into the eighth grade. Then I looked up at Irene. She was crying. Right in front of everybody. She wasn't standing up straight anymore. I wanted to kick that dirty rotten skunk nun, but I was a coward.

Even though Mother stuck up for Irene, later on, back at the party at our house, she didn't stick up for Daddy. While he was carving the meat he told our relatives at the dinner table about not being able to find a Girls' Bathroom in the parish hall. He was spattering blood from the meat on the white tablecloth. Mother was giving him dirty looks from her end of the table, but he didn't see her. He kept carving and saying what he thought about the priests. He said they were in charge of the whole outfit and they wouldn't put in a Girls' Toilet or let women sing in the choir.

Nony and I laughed out loud—Daddy could be so funny without meaning to be. Grandpa Sullivan interrupted Daddy as if he were the head of our house and began to explain why women weren't allowed to say Mass. The first time Grandpa stopped to take a breath, Daddy said, "With all due respect, Grandpa, when you think of how important the kidneys are and what it means once they kick up, a church that doesn't have a women's toilet in it is getting away with murder. Martha was in agony this afternoon . . ."

"I wouldn't exactly call this dinner-table conversation, Henry." Mother's voice sounded like the glass dinner bell.

Irene told me and Nony that Mother knew public school was better than parochial, but a promise is a promise. She said that when Mother and Daddy got married, Mother had to promise the priests she'd send her children to Catholic school. She had to promise that for marrying a non-Catholic like Daddy. I wanted to go to St. Francis Assisi with Nony. In public school you could paint and use clay, but in parochial you learned how to read.

"When the Iroquois Indians tore out all Saint Isaac Joques' fingernails and burned him at the stake, he did not hate the savages. Indeed, he loved them all the more." *That was worse torture than getting crucified. Once you're up there, it couldn't hurt too much.*

"At the age of five, Blessed Imelda longed so much to receive Jesus in Holy Communion that the host flew right out of the priest's hands and stopped over Blessed Imelda's head. So the priest came down from the altar to Blessed Imelda's pew and gave her Communion. She was so happy to have Jesus inside her and she loved Him so much that she died of love right there in her pew. People thought she was only swooning or pretending to be holy." *Wake up, Imelda, this instant, you little faker . . .*

"So determined was Saint Jane Francis de Chantal to serve God completely that when her daughter threw herself down across the threshold as her mother was going out the door to join the convent, Saint Jane walked right over her daughter's body and never looked back." *When mother went out the front door to go to the hospital for her operation I stood in the doorway and kept calling after her and she didn't look back but Irene said she was crying because she was afraid of getting the hysterectomy and because she couldn't teach school anymore . . .*

"When he was a young man, Saint Peter Damien turned his back on the world and went to work among the lepers on the island of Molokai. He came to love the lepers very much, and one day when a hot coal dropped on his foot and he saw it drop but did not feel any pain, he knew that he, too, had leprosy. He was very happy because he knew that God loves the lepers better than healthy people." *Nony says he licked their sores. In* The Book of Heroes and Heroines *he is called Father Damien the Leper, not St. Peter Damien* . . .

Irene and Nony read me stories about great men and women and my mother said Truman was great and Eleanor Roosevelt was very great. Sister Herman Marie told us about the lives of the saints every morning during Religion period. She said everyone, especially the Sisters, was supposed to be perfect like the saints. She was trying to be a perfect first grade teacher. She got perfect by following the *Horarium* perfectly. "Hor-AH-ree-um. Say it, class . . . again . . . Hor-AH-ree-um." That was the Latin word for our daily schedule. It said she had to teach Religion at nine o'clock, Phonics at ten, Arithmetic at ten-thirty, Recess at eleven, and Word Study from eleven-fifteen till lunch time. It was printed in old-fashioned letters and nailed to every classroom wall just above the holy water font. "That way all Monsignor McGoffey or the Principal or any visitor has to do to find out what subject is being taught when they enter any classroom is to look at the *Horarium.*" She said doing the Horarium on time made Jesus happy, but Nony said her teacher upstairs in the fifth grade classroom never looked at it.

Sister Herman Marie hated interruptions. "No questions," she said at the beginning of every Arithmetic lesson. But one morning I couldn't help it. I raised my hand and asked to leave the room to go downstairs to the bathroom.

"Oh, go, baby," she yelled. "I hope everyone in this class knows that only a person with no home training ever says the word "bathroom." I hurried past her and opened the classroom door.

I was almost out the door when she yelled after me, "Come

back here, Miss Bathroom Parade!"

I could see the knuckles on her fists sticking out from under her scapular.

"What should you say when you pass in front of someone, *especially* someone who is in authority over you?"

I looked up at her. I didn't know the answer. I didn't know what she was talking about.

"Haven't you ever heard that when you pass in front of someone, or when you sneeze at table, or disturb someone else in any way at all, the polite person says, 'I beg your pardon, please, Sister Herman Marie.' " Then she walked over to the classroom door and held it open. "Now, get out of here, and stay down in the basement until Recess. I've had enough interruptions from you for one morning."

I ran out the door and forgot to say the password when I went in front of her. I didn't go back when I heard her yelling after me again.

After I came out of the Girls' Bathroom, I went into the main part of the school basement to wait for the class. There were no lights on because there wasn't any class using the basement for Recess. I sat down on a bench and looked up at the big clock over the wooden stage. I heard a noise out where the bathrooms were. It was only Holy Joe, the old caretaker. He was sweeping and talking to himself. He didn't see me.

Then he did something strange. He knocked on the door of the Girls' Bathroom, waited, opened the bathroom door, and went in. I didn't know boys or men were allowed to go into the Girls' Bathroom. We weren't allowed in theirs. I guessed he went in there to fix the toilet that wouldn't stop flushing.

The clock said eleven o'clock by this time, but the class hadn't come down yet. On the other side of the basement were two big doors. They led to the long hallway outside the cafeteria, but today a sign said "WET—Stay Out," and a chair was blocking them. The printing on the sign was very crooked and smudged.

I did not like being down in the basement all by myself. I started to go up to the first stair landing and wait for the class there. But just as I was walking past the Girls' Bathroom, the door opened and Holy Joe came out. I'd seen him go in, but still he scared me coming out unexpectedly like that. He had dribble on his chin. I turned around and walked as fast as I could back into the dim basement and over to the bench.

I tried so hard not to think of it, just the way I tried when I woke up in the middle of the night. Daddy said that if you thought of other, *good* things, soon you'd forget about the bad thing and go back to sleep. But there was nothing good to think about down in that basement. All there was was Holy Joe sweeping the same spot over and over and looking over at me and mumbling and whispering to himself. And so the next time I saw him looking at me, I saw, instead of him, the face of the crazy man in the movie of *The Spiral Staircase* that Irene brought me to when Mother was in the hospital getting her operation and Daddy was visiting her. The man was a killer. He killed everybody he got the chance to kill. He never missed a chance.

Irene had told me lots of times that it was *"only a movie,* dammit." She explained that in real life the killer's name was George Brent. She said if I told Mother and Daddy she'd taken me to see *The Spiral Staircase* she'd get her Italian wrestler boyfriend to break my neck.

In the movie the crazy man hid in closets in a huge dark house with a spiral staircase and when his victims opened the closet door all you saw getting bigger and bigger and bigger till it filled the whole screen—or at night the bedroom—was his one huge crazy Eye. The Eye was filled with his love of killing. You never knew what wall or closet the Eye—his Eye —was going to come out of next. He wanted most of all to kill a poor deaf girl named Dorothy McGuire—she looked like Nony. One night a horrible storm came up and Dorothy got caught alone with him in the big dark house. At first she was not afraid because she did not know George Brent was the killer—during the day when other people were around, he acted like a real gentleman.

I sat there and I tried to convince myself that Holy Joe wouldn't hurt a flea. I thought of how holy he was supposed to be. He yelled his prayers louder than everyone else at Mass. "Lord, have MERCY!" He said it at the wrong times. One time he killed a pigeon that had flown in the round window behind the high altar. He smashed it to bits with his broom, all over the tiles of the middle aisle.

Holy Joe suddenly stopped sweeping.

"Who you lookin' at, girlie?" He looked straight into my eyes.

"The clock." It was quarter after eleven and the class still hadn't come down.

"Why, that's *my* clock, girlie . . . It's three o'clock in the morning." And with that he turned into the Eye.

I didn't wait a second. I pushed the chair out of the way, burst through the double doors with the WET sign, and ran.

Down the long hall, up the stairs three flights to the top floor, through more doors, down another hall, and then right into the fifth grade. "I want Nony," I ran up to the nun and shouted at her. And then I saw my sister over near the window and I ran to her. I was crying, but I didn't care what anybody thought. I knew I was embarrassing Nony, but I climbed into her lap and held onto her.

Her teacher must have run too because in no time she was back with the Principal, Sister Cecilia. She brought me and Nony and her teacher out in the hall and made me tell her what happened. I couldn't stop crying for a long time—I got so scared just telling her about the dark basement and Holy Joe in the bathroom and *The Spiral Staircase.*

Sister Cecilia did not let go of my hand when Sister Herman Marie showed up. Sister Herman Marie explained that she had simply forgotten all about me being down in the basement. She tried to worm her way out of getting blamed by saying she'd forgotten about me because she was rushing to catch up with the Horarium, as my having to go to the Girls' Room off-schedule made her fall behind.

"But my dear Sister," Sister Cecilia said, "your duty is to this child, not to a piece of paper. Some things—your *children* —are much more important than the *Horarium!*"

She was just as nice as Grandma Sullivan to me. She bent down and wiped my face off with her big white handkerchief. She said, "Blow, harder . . ." and then she put my hand in Nony's and sent us home for lunch.

I knew Sister Herman Marie would try to get even with me later on, but I wasn't too afraid of her anymore. The Principal would stick up for me. Sister Herman Marie didn't even know who Harriet Tubman was. When I asked her if she was a saint, Sister said she never heard of her, but if Harriet Tubman was American she couldn't be one, because America had no saints.

Our family was not very holy. We never said the Family Rosary in May or any other time. Mother snored during the sermons on Sunday. Daddy called the May Procession the Ziegfeld Follies. When Nony came home and told that her teacher said that God made Adam and Eve first and after them the priests and nuns because he loves them best of all His children, better than the mothers and fathers, Daddy shouted, "TAKE HER OUT, I want her out of that damn place. She's going to public school." Mother answered him back. Daddy threw down his napkin and went upstairs by himself, before we'd had dessert.

And then, all of a sudden, when it came out of nowhere that Daddy was going to become a Catholic, they acted as if there was nothing strange going on. Here was a grown-up man getting baptized all by himself on a Monday night, not in the regular baptismal font but in a dish in the middle aisle of the church and he did not act embarrassed and my mother talked about the buffet we'd have after Daddy's baptism in the same tone of voice she used to make her Bohack's shopping list on Saturdays: "Let's see, chicken, no, I'll cook a turkey, a ham, that's your father's favorite, and whatever is on sale . . ."

"How come Daddy's gonna be a Catholic when he hates the nuns?" I asked.

"Why, Martha!" Mother said. "That has nothing to do with
it. You ought to know your religion better than that."

I always got in the 90s in Catechism. But I could not understand at all why Daddy wanted to become a convert.

Back home, at the party we had after the ceremony, I found
out a few things that helped me figure out an answer to the
mystery of Daddy's new religion.

The only holy present he got came in the mail from his side
of the family. None of the Girlinghausens would come to the
party because they were all agnostics and atheists. But they
sent the strangest statue of the Blessed Mother holding the
Baby Jesus I'd ever seen. One of the Blessed Mother's breasts
was showing with the pink nipple sticking straight out. The
Baby Jesus was leaning toward it, and both of them were
smiling. The statue said "Rhineland, 15th century" on the
bottom. When Daddy opened it, he looked very happy and he
told everyone standing around that his parents had brought
that statue all the way over from Germany.

Grandma Sullivan's sister who was almost ninety squeaked
out, "Henry! If your father and your mother were Catholic
people, for God's sake, why were you brought up a nothing?"
Daddy said his old man wouldn't give you a plug nickel for
the church after he came to America. I already knew the part
about the priest in Brooklyn who sent a German shepherd
after Daddy's brother because he chased his ball over the
rectory fence. But the night Daddy got baptized was the first
time I heard that Grandpa Girlinghausen had knocked on the
door of the rectory that night and when the priest with the
German shepherd opened it, Grandpa knocked him down. He
got bitten and excommunicated on the spot.

Then Grandpa Sullivan got in his two cents.

"So this thick Dutchman doesn't take it off the water." He had his arm around my father when he said it.

Later on, I was out in the kitchen getting out the cake plates for dessert and I heard Grandma Sullivan giving my mother a piece of her mind.

"He should talk—he's a pretty thick mick himself."

As mother decorated the cake, Grandma said that Grandpa Sullivan had not gone near a church for years back when they lived in the city, because one Sunday the usher at St. Michael's gave her a dirty look for only putting a dime on the collection plate. Mother was drawing vines and leaves and clusters of grapes made out of seven-minute Royal icing all over the sides of the cake and she wasn't paying much attention to Grandma. All she said was "Little pitchers . . ." when Grandma got to the end of her story, which went "After Tommy was born, I was the one who told your father, I said, 'Eddie, you cannot throw the baby out with the bath water.' "

Mother was holding the icing gun very tight now and was concentrating on getting the top of the cake right. As she was pushing out some eighth notes and quarter notes in the staff she'd drawn, Great-Aunt Florrie came out in the kitchen and screamed in her ear, "What's cookin'? Give me a job. I want a job, Gertrude. Let me give you a hand." Mother wouldn't let her get on her nerves because she was starting to draw the G clef. Just as she had almost finished it, Aunt Florrie bumped her elbow against mother's and ruined the clef sign. Mother said, "Oh, *no*," as if she'd been stabbed. Grandma steered Great-Aunt Florrie out of the kitchen. "Too much rum punch," she said to my mother, and Mother raised both eyebrows and said to Grandma, "You see, Mother, it was music that did it for Henry. Thus the cake. I hope I can salvage the G clef."

She did, and after she went inside with the cake, I asked Grandma if she believed in miracles. She said, yes, she did. Why the first thing Grandpa had said after my own mother was born was *"It is a miracle."*

I didn't get to hear many more words that night. While Mother was cutting the beautiful cake for the relatives, I had to go down the cellar and bring up the Mary Margaret McBride rosebushes we were giving Daddy for his present. After the cake I had to go to bed because the next day was school. From my bed upstairs I did hear them all singing around the piano as if it were just another party. Mother and Daddy sang a duet to "And We Will Row, Row, Row." Daddy didn't sound one bit different now that he was Catholic, except that it was the first time I'd ever heard him sing popular music—usually he only liked classical.

But if I had had a diary, I would still have written in it that Daddy's new religion was a mystery, pure and simple. There is no understanding why a person goes and gets baptized at the age of forty-six. Maybe he was lonesome when we went to Mass on Sundays, but I don't think so because when we came home he was always happy from listening to his records. In fact he acted happier than we did. Maybe he was afraid of going to hell.

But I didn't keep a diary because Nony and Irene would have read it. I know because Irene and I always read Nony's until Nony found out and tried to kill me with Daddy's carving knife. As I said, our family was not a holy one.

Christmas, I thought, was the most perfect time of year. I thought if I let on I didn't believe in Santa Claus anymore, I'd spoil it. And I liked watching everyone pretend Santa was coming again, as if there was still a baby in our house.

All through Advent, Mother stashed presents in the back of her closet. She kept it locked, she said, so the cat couldn't deposit her new litter of kittens in her shoes. At night I heard her trying to get Daddy into the Christmas spirit.

"Henry, you must get started on that bassinet for Martha."

"Have a heart, Gertrude. I'm all in. It's gotta be a bassinet, huh?"

"That's the only thing she wants. Just attach some legs to the old car basket we used when they were babies. I can make the skirt in no time. It's probably her last Christmas for believing in Santa Claus."

"Anything for our littlest angel," Daddy said, yawning.

On Christmas Eve he came home from his office party late for dinner and, as Mother said, "feeling no pain." I knew from snooping around his workbench in the cellar that he hadn't started my bassinet. On my way upstairs to bed as I passed through the living room, I saw him kneeling on the floor holding his chest and looking at the tree he had just screwed into the stand. He had put it in crooked and the bare spot was gaping right out into the living room instead of being hidden around the back. I wanted to say, "Forget about the bassinet, Dad, and go to bed. I don't believe anyway."

Instead, I listened from our bedroom upstairs and heard him sawing off the bottom of the tree trunk, vacuuming up the sawdust, wrestling up the tree again, cursing. He calmed down when he wound the lights onto the branches because I could hear him singing:

> *Stille nacht!*
> *Heilige nacht!*

I could smell the stöllen baking too. It had been rising all afternoon.

I woke up in the middle of the night. In her twin bed Nony was reading by flashlight and sniffling. I watched her wipe her nose with the sheet.

"Did Santa Claus come yet?" I whispered.

"Sh!"

Her eyes glowed like cats' eyes in the beam of the flashlight. Nony knew how to make just the whites of her eyes show.   .

Finally, she shut the book with a bang, said "Finished," and threw it on the floor.

"What was it?"

"The life of Mozart. He died when he was thirty-five and they buried him in a pauper's grave even though he was a genius. He wrote his first symphony when he was only five years old." She was talking loud.

"Oh," I whispered. Daddy's favorite composer was Mozart.

Then Nony said we didn't have to whisper because Mother and Daddy and Irene were out at Midnight Mass. She was playing her flashlight in zigzaggy lines all over the ceiling and up and down the closet door.

"You don't really believe in Santa Claus, do you?" Nony said.

Nony always knew when I was lying. I told her the truth. Then we made a bargain that we'd tell each other our presents right then, but we had to promise to make believe they were surprises in the morning and never to tell on each other.

"There's nothing wrong with it," she said. "It's Christmas already. It's way after midnight."

I told her she was getting *My Antonía,* a dress, and skates, and then, as she started telling me about the bassinet Mother and Daddy were making for me, I lay there thinking this is a rotten bargain because I already know what I'm getting. When we heard the front door open and mother call out, "Oh, Henry, smell the pine!" we made believe we were fast asleep like the pair of cheats we were.

Mother and Daddy worked all night on the bassinet. I heard Daddy going up and down stairs time after time, tripping over empty Evervess bottles on the cellar stairs, looking for his drill, telling Mother his lousy, cheap drill had come apart in his goddamn hands. Mother made the house hum as she floored the sewing machine pedal, trying to finish the skirt by Christmas morning. I got up to go to the bathroom once, and as I passed their bedroom, I saw her leaning over the machine and the bedroom floor swimming in pink and white material, as if their room was one soft wave of pink and white. Mother loved to make things. Lots of times she worked all night to finish one of her "projects" in time for a special occasion. When Daddy tried to get her to go to bed, she'd say, "There'll be plenty of time for sleep in the grave!"

Usually, the first one to wake up on Christmas morning woke everybody else up, provided it was after six o'clock. Daddy would go downstairs first and plug in the tree lights and turn on the record of "Silent Night." Then Mother and the three of us would come down with our presents for one another. The venetian blinds would still be closed from the night before. With only the tree lights on in the living room it felt like the middle of the night and as if it was snowing outside.

But this Christmas was different right from the beginning. When I went in to wake up Mother and Daddy at six-thirty, they sent me back to bed for another half hour. When Nony went in the next time, they said, "Just one more half hour, *please.*" By the time Mother got up, it was broad daylight. Daddy didn't move. Mother told us he would get up when everything was ready. She went downstairs to turn on the tree lights. When she called up that we could come down now, Daddy opened his eyes and mumbled, "Go on, I'll be right down."

Downstairs, everything looked pretty much the way it always did on Christmas except that Mother had opened the blinds. There was no feeling at all that it might be the middle of the night and snowing outside. Inside and out, everything looked gray, except for the corner where the tree lights were shining red and green and royal blue. But without Daddy there, it all felt flat. While we looked at our presents very politely, Mother kept going back and forth to the foot of the stairs and calling up in a very patient tone of voice, "Henry, we're all ready. The children are waiting, Henry . . ."

They never wrapped the things under the tree that Santa Claus was supposed to have left. So after a little while we had seen all our presents, but we were holding back, not making a fuss about anything until he came down. Irene said we could look in our stockings while we were waiting for him. I went over to the fireplace and was taking the thumb tack out of my stocking that was tacked into the mantelpiece. All of a sudden over my head I heard the sound of knocking coming through the living room ceiling. Then it stopped. The next time it came, the four of us heard it. "Maybe Daddy wants us to be quiet so he can sleep," I said. With that I heard a voice I'd never heard before calling downstairs, "Gertrude . . . Gertrude . . . come up."

Mother ran. Irene stood at the foot of the stairs, listening. Nony and I kept looking at our presents, not saying anything. Nothing under the tree was a surprise for either of us. The most beautiful present there, by far, was the bassinet. It looked good enough for a real baby. The tree lights shone like circles of rainbow on the white skirt. Around the top, where the skirt was gathered, there was a band of baby blue ribbon. At the foot of the basket, it was tied in a big bow with streamers hanging down to the floor. I lifted up the pink underskirt and I saw the legs and the four wheels that Daddy had taken off my old kiddie cart.

Then Mother came to the head of the stairs and clicked her fingers. "Irene, come up," she said in a very low voice. A few seconds later she came downstairs herself and went out to the kitchen. She closed the door, but Nony and I listened to her dial the phone and then ask for Dr. Whitehead.

"This is Gertrude Girlinghausen, Mrs. Whitehead. I am sorry to call on Christmas morning, but Henry thinks he is having a heart attack. His color is as green as the Christmas tree."

Before Nony and I could get out of the way of the kitchen door, Mother hung up and swung it open. She didn't notice that she almost sent me through the dining room wall. She dashed through the living room, as if she were in charge of a fire drill, and back upstairs. Then Irene came down and put a pot of water on the stove. Just as it started to boil, the doorbell rang and Dr. Whitehead came and ran upstairs without taking off his coat.

Nony and I tried to hear what was going on from the downstairs hall, but there wasn't a sound from Mother and Daddy's bedroom. Once, the doctor ran downstairs and through the living room out to the kitchen and then back upstairs again.

Nony stood at the bottom of the stairs crying but holding in the noise. She said, "Daddy is going to die." She sounded like she'd like to kill someone. Watching her cry, I remembered the time Mother always told about—I was three and almost died and Nony had knelt in front of a statue all day shouting "God! Don't you let my baby sister die. If you do, I'll hate you, God." I thought any minute she might start warning God again, she was crying so hard and looked so mad. I knew Daddy was not going to die. When we put up the storm windows on Election Day, he carried five at a time up from the cellar. He could lift the piano all by himself. He could run from our house to the Long Island Railroad station

in 9½ minutes. Up in Saugerties, he carried me on his back
for three miles in the rain. Then I thought I'd better say a
prayer for him just in case. "Please, God, let there be a miracle. After all, it is Christmas."

When Mother came downstairs, she told us what we'd
heard her say over the phone except that this time she said
Daddy had definitely had a heart attack. The doctor didn't
know yet if Daddy would make it. She went back upstairs and
never left their bedroom till Christmas was over. The rest of
the day only Irene went up and down carrying trays and giving
reports—Dr. Whitehead would say no more than "It's touch
and go." Flushing Hospital came with oxygen, Nony made
dinner and I tidied up the living room. When I ran the carpet
sweeper over the rug, it didn't pick up any dirt, so I took it
out on the back stoop where the garbage pails were to clean
it out. I opened it on top of a piece of newspaper. A big wad
of dust full of pink and white scraps fell out in one neat piece.
The scraps were left over from the skirt of my bassinet. I
picked out a few to put in my wallet, behind Daddy's picture,
in case he died. If he does die, I thought, I did it—by making
believe about Santa Claus and forcing Daddy to kill himself all
night long over a bassinet. When Billy Hayes' mother died,
I remembered as I smoothed out one scrap of pink material
and one of white, he put pennies over her eyes in the coffin
and his father slapped him dizzy.

It was dark out before Nony and I were allowed to go
upstairs. I expected Daddy to have his eyes closed and look
like a corpse. But as I stood staring at him from the foot of
their four-poster, I thought no one would ever guess he had

almost died and still might. He smiled at Nony and me and cracked jokes about being sick and about how quiet the house was—no fights, no music—he thought something was wrong downstairs. Then he asked me what Santa Claus had had to show for himself. I described the bassinet without looking at Nony. While I talked, Mother was holding Daddy's hand. Usually they bickered a lot, about the check book and whether Harry Truman was good or bad, but now they looked brand new, like lovers. Then Daddy asked if his three Christmas angels would give him some music on the piano. We went downstairs and Nony played his favorite carol, "Lo, How A Rose E'er Blooming." Irene played a piece by Bach—she said it was some music by Bach that had made Daddy decide to be baptized. I played "The Happy Farmer" by Robert Schumann, but I made mistakes because in the middle of it Nony shouted out, "It's snowing!" and I couldn't help looking out the window while I was playing.

The snow came down all night long. In the morning it was still pouring out of the sky as if the sky couldn't get enough of giving the old bare bones world a snow feast. On the kitchen radio John Gambling said the blizzard of December 26, 1947, would go down in history. He talked about how "heavenly" Central Park had looked when he passed it on his way to the WOR studio. He made "New York under a blanket of snow" sound like a miracle. Our street looked like one, it was so changed. There wasn't a sign of a garbage pail or a car.

Mother said the three of us had to start shoveling right after breakfast. Flushing Hospital would be delivering a hospital bed and a stretcher if they could get through. It was too risky to move Daddy to the hospital, but the doctor said he could be moved into a hospital bed in his own house. Mother said he stood a much better chance in his own home than in a hospital, but the next ten days or so would tell the story. "Dr. Whitehead says Daddy must have absolute peace and quiet," she said. "There is to be no arguing, no tattle-taling, not one fight."

We shoveled all morning. We were a good team. Once in a while we threw snowballs, but there wasn't time to fool around much. The hospital phoned to say as soon as the streets were plowed, they'd deliver the bed. We had to finish fast. The snow stopped falling in early afternoon. The wind died down and the sun came out. The sky was robin's-egg blue and there were bright blue sparkles dancing everywhere. Irene looked like a hunter in her red hood. Nony's cheeks were flaming red. Her dark eyes flashed as bright as the black jet buttons on Irene's winter coat. My big sisters, they were dark-eyed, rosy snowgirls.

Then, out of nowhere, snowballs came flying at us. They were packed hard. The first one hit Irene on the forehead and made her bleed. I picked it up. It was packed with a rock inside of it. The only moving things in sight were some sparrows and, about ten blocks away, the first snowplow. The second we went back to our shoveling, the bombardment started again. Irene held her arms up like a shield and hid her head behind them and finally she spotted them. Three boys were crouched down behind a snow bank in the lot on the far corner of Myrtle Avenue.

"Oh!" Nony cried. "It's George Egan, Irene, and Peter Reifstanger from my class. I don't know the other one." She sounded glad to see them.

"You big babies," I screamed across the street. "Why don't

you come out in the open and fight?" I took aim.

But, as Irene got hit in the chest, she yelled at me, "Put that down, Martha. They'll stop if you ignore them. All they want is attention." Irene had a bloody nose by this time, but she was forbidding me to fight back.

Two of the boys held their fire when they saw us not doing anything. But George Egan kept sending one snowball after another over our heads and hitting the roof of our house. He was pitching them as hard and mean as he could. From inside our house it must have sounded like it was hailing baseballs. All of a sudden I thought of Daddy lying upstairs with his heart attack and wondering what the hell was landing on the roof. "Cut it out, you coward," I screamed at Egan. He was the biggest of the three.

But he only lowered his aim. Now he was firing snowballs at the side of the dormer that jutted out from the second story of the house. In the dormer were two small windows. My parents' bed—Daddy—was directly under those windows. If Egan broke one of those windows with a snowball, the shock and the falling glass could kill Daddy.

Irene and Nony saw how dangerous it was too. But when Irene started to walk toward the lot to explain to them about our father lying under the window with his heart attack, Egan threw a snowball and hit her on the temple. She was stunned. He laughed like crazy and jumped up and down as if he'd made a triple homer. In church Egan always looked like St. Aloysius, Boy Saint. He was Monsignor's favorite altar boy and even though he was in high school he still came back to carry the gold cross in all the big processions. He was as tall as the priests and everyone knew he wanted to be one himself someday. His big sister was a nun.

We could see him packing a new round fast and stacking them in triangles like cannonballs. He was getting ready for a long siege. Peter Reifstanger and the other kid were resting, but Egan started firing with blood in his eye.

I plunged across the street, through the snow that came up to my waist. I screamed at the top of my lungs, "You g.d. hypocrite, Egan . . . you *bitch!*" Irene had called me that once and got beat with an umbrella.

It stopped him. He dropped his snowball and marched out of the lot and across Myrtle Avenue toward our driveway. The only sound was the snowplow that was almost up to our street. Then, as he got to our property, he shouted that no little twerp was calling him filthy names and getting away with it. He was in a rage. Irene tried to explain to him about Daddy's bed being under the windows, but Egan said that had nothing "whatsoever" to do with him. "If I have to break down your front door and tell your father myself what this little pig called me, I'll make him make you apologize, heart attack or no heart attack." The snowplow was now in front of our house making a racket.

I tried to lie my way out of the whole thing, but he pushed me out of his way, said I was a liar as well as a pig, and started up our driveway toward the front door. We ran to keep him off the stoop, but before we could stop him he had his hand on the knocker. Nony was yelling, "Our father almost died yesterday and he still might, you can ask anybody," but Egan was already banging the knocker. Irene was big enough to knock him off the stoop, but instead of using her muscles she tried to talk him out of it.

"My mother is not available, George, and my father is quite ill. I'm the person in charge today, so will you accept an apology from me?" He had started the war, yet here she was acting guilty.

"Get off our property or we'll call the police," I said.

Egan pointed his finger at me and said to Irene, "Your sister here is no good, I hope you know that." He rapped the knocker three more times. "She's a no good liar and a no good pig."

If I felt scared, I will never forget how scared he looked when all of a sudden the truck from Flushing Hospital pulled into our driveway and two huge Negro men hopped out and began to unload the parts of a brown iron bed. As they came up the driveway carrying the spring, we moved out of their way, but Egan didn't budge from the doorway. They hollered, "Step aside, boy." Egan moved back then, too far—he slipped on the snow and off the stoop, flat on his can. I laughed at him in that real nasty way that is called jeering. When Egan got out to the sidewalk, he picked up some snow. He threw the first snowball at me, but I ducked in time, and then he shouted "Pig" at me as he threw another one through our open front door. He must have gone snow-blind because one of the delivery men was coming out the door as Egan threw the snowball. Egan hit him. The delivery man started after him, but then he gave up right away. You could tell he thought Egan was just a stupid kid, not worth a good chase. As he hauled a stretcher out of the back of the truck, I heard him say, "That some chickenshit, man!"

"Chickenshit!" It was the perfect nickname.

Ordinarily, Irene would have tattled on me for using bad language in public and I would have gotten my mouth washed out with Swan's soap. But for Daddy's sake, she kept her mouth shut. Mother spent Christmas vacation taking care of him. When he slept, she did her Plan Book. Dr. Whitehead said she had to be a teacher again because Daddy couldn't work for a long time. Nony and I did the shopping, Irene cooked, and we all kept the house in order. At night we ate dessert upstairs in Mother and Daddy's room and no one was allowed to tell anything unpleasant. When Daddy asked if his office had phoned, Nony said, "No, Daddy," so sweetly, as if she was The Little Flower and could not tell a lie. Everyone except him knew that his crumby boss had fired him when he heard about the heart attack, but we just smiled as if life was as lovely as the snowy streets outside. Daddy said this snow was almost as bad as the blizzard of 1888, when his mother and father had come over from Germany to get away from Bismarck, that g.d. Prussian.

On the Feast of the Epiphany, which Irene called "Three Kings Day" and Nony "the Twelfth Day of Christmas," Dr. Whitehead said Daddy was "out of the woods." He would not die right now, though he might only have five good years left. It depended on how well he could manage with the "bum valve"—the attack had done permanent damage to one of the valves in his heart. My escape was as narrow as Daddy's. I had put a hole in his heart, but I hadn't killed him. The doctor called Daddy "Miracle Man."

He said he was now strong enough to have the priest. The doctor hadn't wanted him to receive the Sacrament of Extreme Unction at the time of the attack because he said sometimes the patient got the wrong idea when he heard the priest praying over him, "Go forth, O Christian soul, out of this world, in the name of God, the Father Almighty." But now that the ten-day danger period had passed, he said it would be okay if the priest brought Communion. Irene called it "Holy Viaticum," Nony said it was not, it was "Communion of the Sick."

Whatever it was, we had to kneel on the bedroom floor around the hospital bed while the priest did his business. No one knew where to look, we were all embarrassed. I stared at my bassinet which I had brought upstairs sometime during Christmas week and wheeled to the foot of their four-poster bed. Then I stared at the priest's hands. I watched him open and close the pyx and take out the host with the cleanest fingernails I ever saw. After he finished giving out Communion, while he was packing up his sacramentals, he asked Daddy why he thought he had had a heart attack. Daddy said something about too much Christmas and then he pointed to the bassinet. "That's the thing that almost finished me," he said. Mother cut in quickly. "Henry gave *Santa Claus* a little assistance this year, Father, assembling the bassinet for Martha, our *youngest* daughter."

"It's okay," I said. It was time to stop faking, I'd ruined enough. "I know about Santa Claus now."

"Why, what do you mean, Martha?"

"I mean it's—he's—for kids. I don't mean there isn't any. He's just different than I used to think." Daddy should have died, according to what the doctor saw on his cardiogram. But he didn't, because, I thought, his heart attack happened on Christmas. Santa Claus, or something connected with Christmas, had saved him. And saved me.

"Christmas won't be the same without Santa Claus, will it, Henry? Without any little children in the house . . ." Mother sounded sad and looked at me as if I'd done something wrong.

Daddy just laughed and said good riddance.

2

Rosie O'Grady could punch a ball as far as any boy and we hung around together. She could climb over the twenty-foot chain fence around Bowne Park playground before the parkie could put down his broom and shout, "Off that fence!" Outside of school she said "ain't" and "Him and her can't do nothin'," but on her report cards she got at least 96 in English and every other subject without half trying. Her homework was always done on time, neat and perfect, but she never wasted afternoons on it. Running home from school to do homework instead of getting out of your uniform and onto your bike was for fags. In Flushing anyone who kept the rules with a straight face and did not do exactly what everyone else did—play ball, ride bikes, get thrown out of the Kiddie Show on Saturdays—such goody-goodies were called fags. (Because she had never smoked in the lots and always wore her uniform hat to high school, I was afraid Nony might be a fag.) There was nothing faggy about Rosie.

She was the oldest of seven children, all girls. The only job she had to do after school was mind one or two of the little sisters. While we played ball, Mary or Sheila or Maureen O'Grady sat on a curb and ate the peanuts we bought her in Sam's. By the time each O'Grady kid was four, she could fill in when we were short a player. The O'Gradys lived in a crowded apartment on a dead-end street the other side of Northern Boulevard. I loved Rosie's street. It was full of kids from the apartment houses all playing punch ball like pros. Where I lived the neighbors made Dicky Johnson take his basketball hoop off the telephone pole because of the noise, and if you ran on their lawns playing Spud they made more noise than we did screaming at us. The first time after I played in her street, Rosie showed me a shortcut back to my neighborhood. You had to cross the Long Island Railroad tracks, climb up the banks, and crawl under a barbed wire fence before the stationmaster at Depot Road caught you or you fell on broken glass. When I got back to our house and my mother asked what Rosie's place was like and how in the world did they ever manage all those children in four rooms, I could tell she thought we were better off than the O'Gradys.

The nuns liked Rosie the best of all the girls in the class, and the three cutest boys had her for their girl friend. She liked Big Toomey best, so they were a couple. Me and Quirk were a couple too, for 2½ years. The four of us never talked to one another when we got together, we just teased or crashed our bikes into each other and wrote "How are you, I am fine" notes in the summer. The class found out we were definitely couples when the Principal called the four of us down to her office over the loudspeaker. Someone had informed her that me and Rosie and Big Toomey and Quirk were going on a real date to the Rodeo in Madison Square Garden on Saturday afternoon. She wanted to know if our parents approved of such an "expedition," especially in Lent. Rosie's did, she said, and so did the boys'. My mother wasn't around to stop me. Every spring she had to go to the hospital for observation and sometimes for an operation on her back—the doctors said with a back like hers she never should have had any babies. Daddy didn't see anything wrong with letting me go on a class outing to the Planetarium. If I had told him about going on a date to the Rodeo, he would have discussed it with Mother and the answer would have been no.

From the time we first started hanging around together Rosie and I had planned to walk into Manhattan someday instead of taking the faggy subway. We had thought we'd have to wait till we were in high school. Both of us wanted to go to a high school in the "city" rather than a faggy one near home in Queens. But when we still had a few years left of grammar school, Quirk and Toomey asked us to the Rodeo. Rosie thought fast and said, "Sure—only let's walk." They didn't act like they found the idea too exciting, but they didn't refuse.

To get to the Garden in time for the noon matinee, we figured we should meet in front of the church at four o'clock in the morning. Lucky for me my father was sound asleep when I snuck out of the house at three-thirty. He never would have bought the idea of a class outing to the city that went on foot in the middle of the night. My crinoline slip made a starchy noise when I walked and my shoes had leather heels, so I carried them downstairs and out the back door and put

them on out in the driveway under the moon. Even from her
hospital bed my mother could make me dress up like Alice
Blue Gown. She had told Daddy to make sure I wore last
year's Easter outfit on the class trip to the Planetarium. Over
the phone she told me, "By no means set foot out that door
in sneakers and jeans. I do not care who else in your class is
doing it." She was referring to Rosie. Rosie never wore a
dress except when she absolutely had to: on Sundays and Holy
Days of Obligation. If I got home from the Rodeo that afternoon wearing jeans, I'd get killed and besides that I might
make him suspicious about where I had really been. So I
showed up in front of St. Francis' church in waffle piqué and
patent-leather pumps looking like I was about to lead a May
procession, instead of walking into the biggest city in the
world.

For Rosie, the eleven-mile trek from Flushing to the East
River was a cinch. Like a champion she took block after block
down Northern, through Murray Hill, and then along Roosevelt Avenue under the giant el that linked Flushing Main
Street and Times Square. She didn't get a bit puffed up that
once again she was the best. She didn't make fun of us for
wanting to stop for Cokes. As we started into Corona, she
didn't blink. After we got out of Flushing and past Willets
Point, I felt a little nervous about going through that neighborhood in the dark because it was mostly Negro. My father
always blamed it on La Guardia. *Back in the thirties he brought
them up from the South in busloads and dumped them in Corona of
all the dead-end places, without a hope of a job, the whole time acting
as if he was helping them . . .* When we saw the lights on inside
a candy store and a Negro man standing in the doorway, I

wanted to keep going and wait till we got to Jackson Heights to stop, but Quirk said, "C'mon, here. There might not be another place open for hours." It was only about five o'clock. The clock on the tower with the Serval Zipper sign said twenty of six when we crossed the smelly Flushing River.

Rosie played handball up against a wall while we sat on the curb of 111 Street under the el and the man in the doorway hummed. Rosie never rested once. By the time we finished the Cokes and Big Toomey had devoured three Clark Bars, the dawn had come. Looking up through the tracks and iron pillars of the el you could see the sky getting bright and a few morning stars still shining. The candy store man stopped humming and told us we were lucky we'd stopped at his place because his was the only all-night joint in Queens. Then he said, "Now Kansas City is another story." He started whistling so loud the sound reached as high as the el and as far as you could see the rusty iron arcade stretching under it, back toward the Willets Point junk yards and ahead toward the city.

If my father could have seen Corona at dawn he never would have called it a slum. Walking west, down the middle of Roosevelt Avenue, we passed rows of tall houses on steep terraces overlooking gardens of sunflowers. When there weren't sunflowers there were magnolia trees just blooming and lawns made out of myrtle and pachysandra, not grass. Quirk was a good whistler too and he kept something going all the way from 111 Street to Junction Boulevard. Then the first train of the morning passed overhead and after the junction the neighborhood became mostly stores and bars and banks along both sides of the street. In the morning with not a soul in sight—just the four of us and the old trolley tracks and the cobblestones straight ahead going all the way to the East River, with lines and squares and rectangles of sunlight all over them—even Jackson Heights looked good. I had always heard Jackson Heights was blah, nothing but apartments.

Once in a while a taxi came toward us from the city and we had to move over into one lane. Quirk said the cabs were bringing home the drunks. At the corner of Seventy-fourth Street, where lots of streets intersected and a cab was stopped for the light, he went up to the passengers' window, looked inside, and made the "Kiss My Ass in Macy's Window" sign at the man and woman in the back seat. But mostly Quirk dropped behind because he was checking his pockets. Every few blocks he took all the money out of the back pocket of his gray Sunday slacks and counted it. He'd no sooner catch up with us than three blocks later there he'd be three blocks behind counting his dollar bills.

With hardly any traffic Toomey made believe there were basketball hoops on every pillar of the el. He kept practicing jump shots. He looked like an acrobat springing up in and out of the dirty rays of sun shining down through the el. By the time we got to Woodside, my good shoes were killing me and the horsehair of my crinoline was scratching the insides of my knees so bad they were bleeding a little. Rosie hadn't broken stride once in her old sneakers that looked so comfortable. For the first time I noticed she was pigeon-toed in her left foot. I let her and Toomey get ahead of me while Quirk was safely counting away back on the steps of St. Sebastian's Church. Ducking into the doorway of a store that had drums and guitars in the window, I took off the horsehair slip. Then I stuffed it into a trash can at the corner of Fifty-ninth Place. I wanted to shout "Slow down" to Rosie. We were more than halfway there and it was still six hours till the Rodeo. I could see she didn't look left or right in the store windows or even at the three or four strange people who came out of nowhere along the way. Rosie had wonderful powers of concentration. She always said she could get her homework done any place she found room in the house, even though the Giants might be on television.

I thought I was the only one who saw the old lady curled up in the doorway next to Doherty's Bar in Sunnyside. She had gone to the bathroom all over herself and was lying in it. Except that she was all beat up, she looked like my grandmother. I stood there looking at her and I didn't know how to help her out. She was snoring. I couldn't think of a thing to do. If I tried to drag her out of the doorway onto the sidewalk where a cop would see her, I'd get the stuff all over me. I went on and waited for Quirk at the next corner. I felt stinking to go off and leave her there like that. But when Quirk came along he said Sunnyside had cost him a buck; he'd seen a drunk back there and had given her money for a cab. That was something, better than nothing.

Rosie and Toomey waited for us at the Fifty-ninth Street Bridge. We'd come all that way on our own speed, but for a minute it looked like we couldn't get out of Queens without using some kind of transportation besides our legs. The sign on the lower roadway said "Queensboro Bridge, No Pedestrians." I said no one would ever have to know if we just took the bus across the bridge and got right off on the other side. Toomey said we could cut down through the freight yards and sneak through the Midtown Tunnel. His cousins in the Bronx

walked through the subway tunnels all the time. All you had
to do when the train or cars came through was stand flat
against the wall. Quirk wanted to risk getting caught and take
the bridge. He said, "If a cop comes along, all you have to do
is say, 'My father's a cop' and they'll let you alone. It works
when they catch you with firecrackers. They're really stupid."
Rosie had the best solution. She led us around blocks and
blocks of warehouses to the upper level of the bridge. Her
uncle lived in Astoria so she knew the neighborhood.

There was no sign, so we started over. There was no walk-
way either. Rosie said the Queensboro stunk, all the other
New York bridges had lanes for pedestrians. She'd walked
over all of them with her Uncle Nicky. We went up the ramp
fast in single file. At the top when we got to the bridge itself,
Quirk stopped and leaned over the railing to spit in the East
River. He said he never passed up a new river without spitting
in it. He wanted to see all the big rivers in the world; maybe
someday he'd be a sailor. From the bridge New York looked
like a city in heaven, towering over a river of tugs and bridges
and swirling currents. I made believe I was an explorer laying
claim to the territory as we filed down and around the sharp
bend of the ramp and into the empty streets of Manhattan.

Toomey must have been thinking about pioneers too because when he saw an open restaurant he whooped like an
Indian and did a war dance in the middle of Lexington Avenue. When the waitress tried to take his order, instead of
speaking to her, he pointed to what he wanted on the menu
and said "Ugh" for each thing he showed her. After breakfast
he whistled down a taxi and after we got in he said to the
driver, "Times, ugh, Square, ugh ugh." Then he whooped

like a maniac, so the cabbie slammed on his brakes and shouted back at him, "Shad up, or get out and walk, Tonto." As we were passing St. Patrick's Cathedral, Rosie said in a weak voice, "I think I am going to vomit." The cabbie screeched to another stop, a full one this time, and inside of ten seconds he had dumped us on the sidewalk. After he drove off without making us pay, Rosie said she wasn't sick at all, she was just fooling around. She'd heard the best way to get a seat on the subway was to say you were going to throw up, very loud so everyone near you could hear. Toomey thought that was a riot. The way he looked at her you could tell he liked her and was glad she was his date.

Since we were right there, Rosie wanted to go inside the cathedral. It was the day before Passion Sunday so there was purple draped all over everything. Rosie went back to see the Lady Chapel and I got hysterical watching Toomey and Quirk run in and out of confessionals marked "Spanish" and "German" and "French." A priest with a beard came out of a "Spanish" one and chased Quirk all the way down the side aisle and out onto Fifth Avenue. I hid in a dark room in the vestibule where they sold pamphlets till he went back in his box. When Rosie came along we went out on the steps where the boys were scaring pigeons. Then we started over toward Times Square. We had three hours to kill before the Rodeo started.

First we sat on the square across from the Crossroads Café and watched the characters. Then we fooled around in a few shooting galleries and played the pinball machines, but after we got thrown out of a joint next to Roseland (Rosie said the guy bounced us because I was dressed up like such a fag), we walked up and down Broadway.

It was while we were looking up at the Gordon's Gin billboard that everything went blank. Quirk started holding my hand. We walked along the sidewalk and over the subway grates and he held it and swung it and wasn't embarrassed. It was my first time doing anything. For the seventh grade, our class was slow. There hadn't yet been one boy and girl party though most of us had taken dancing lessons at the Knights of Columbus. The nuns said your First Communion Day was supposed to be the happiest day of your life, but they probably never roamed through Times Square holding hands with one of the cutest boys in the class. Rosie saw our hands but she looked away fast and kept her mouth shut. She and Toomey weren't doing anything.

Inside Madison Square Garden, I went into our row first and Rosie came in right behind me instead of letting Quirk go next. Maybe she didn't know that dates were supposed to sit together. He wound up at the other end from me. Rosie and Toomey sat snug in the middle, side by side. Once the Rodeo started, though, it didn't matter. The cowboys were concentrating so hard they made you concentrate even if you didn't know what a Rodeo was all about. Watching them throw their ropes and hang on to the bucking broncos reminded me of the way the conductors looked at the summer concerts at Lewisohn Stadium, as if they wouldn't care if they died on stage as long as the violins came in at the right time. If they heard the sirens of the ambulances and the shrieking fire engines in the streets outside the stadium, they never let on. All through the Rodeo, I forgot that I was on my first date. I sat there wondering if when I grew up I'd be able to think of something to be that was like being a conductor or a cowboy, something you couldn't live without doing.

On the way home on the IRT, Quirk and Big Toomey rode between the cars, Rosie read the funnies someone had left behind on a seat, and I stood looking out the window, at the city skyline in the distance, beyond the low roofs of Queens.

Monica Sheridan gave our class's first boy and girl party exactly one week after the Rodeo, the Saturday night before Palm Sunday to be exact. The kissing games were more fun than the dancing. Only Quirk could ask me to dance because we were a couple, but at Post Office and Spin-the-Bottle you got a chance to kiss a lot of people and compare. Some boys closed their eyes, some put their hands on your shoulders, and Freddie Hart just kissed me on the cheek like a friend. A few boys acted like creeps when the bottle stopped on someone they didn't like, and Big Toomey would only go in the closet with Rosie. Once we timed them the way we did one another on the confession line. Monica opened the door when sixty seconds were up and Big Toomey came out purple, wiping his mouth and chin. Rosie's face and neck were covered with red blotches which Monica called "beard burn." Monica could get away with acting wiser than anybody else about boy and girl stuff because she was the first girl in our class to wear a bra. In her school uniform her figure looked like Miss Rheingold's. Rosie's chest was beginning to flop when she ran, but even when Monica did Irish jigs up on the stage at Assembly, hers didn't budge. I didn't have a thing yet, so I stuffed my shirt with toilet paper. Nobody, not even Rosie, knew mine were fake.

Monica also knew the facts of life. She said she saw her parents "do it" on the kitchen table when she was seven. That was how old I was when I read about Dr. Kinsey's report in the *Star Journal.* Ever since, I'd been trying to get my mother to explain the facts, but I never seemed to ask her the right questions. I didn't know how much Rosie knew; all I knew was that women have wombs. I figured that out from the Hail Mary: "And blessed is the fruit of thy womb, Jesus!" Soon I was going to know more than anybody. Irene was engaged to be married (though Daddy said she'd marry Steve over his dead body, Steve was such a stiff) and I'd wheedle the facts out of her.

Our teacher, Sister Richard Dolores, was not married, of course, but she beat Irene to it. She told all the girls in the class to come to school an hour before the procession started on Holy Thursday and we knew she was going to talk about the boys because she'd found some notes in the trash basket about Monica's party and the kissing games. Dicky Dee, as we called her, was very popular—she was the only nun in St. Francis who would roll up the sleeves of her habit out in the play yard and shoot a basketball.

She began by telling us we didn't have to take our regular seats in the classroom or put our wraps in the press because we only had forty minutes before Solemn High Mass. After every girl had found a desk—I chose Quirk's and Rosie Big Toomey's—she told us how disappointed she'd been to find out what a fresh bunch of girls we were turning into. There was a time when she'd thought we were very mature. She scolded those of us who'd gone to Miss Sheridan's party, not just for playing kissing games but for breaking the spirit of

Lent. "What kind of women will you become if you're going to parties in Lent now?" And then she told us blow by blow.

There was nothing wrong with what she was about to tell us, since God created it, but He created it for our mothers and fathers. "When your mom and dad wanted to have you, they lay on the bed together, and cuddled up very close to one another. Your dad held your mother very tight, and then he took the organ called his penis and put it in the hole your mothers have between their legs. You can't see the hole because on adults it is covered up with what is called pubic hair."

I shot a fast look over at Monica who was keeping a straight face. Most kids were looking down at their white gloves or staring hard at the inkwells. There was no telling who was hearing the facts for the first time and who already knew them. Rosie was looking up at Dicky Dee as if she was Our Lady of Lourdes and Rosie was St. Bernadette.

"Your dad's seed comes out of his penis and goes into your mother like an injection and that seed grows inside her womb for nine months. Then the baby is ready to come out. This is the same way that dogs make puppies, sheep lambs, and so on. Penis into hole, seed into baby. When you get married, you and your husbands will have sexual intercourse the same way your moms and dads do now. It's the way God made for all people to have children. Out of love for Him alone, however, priests and sisters are a special group of people who stay chaste like the Blessed Virgin Mary. A virgin is someone who never has sexual intercourse for the love of God. At the Last Judgment, the virgins and martyrs will receive their crowns before married people, but that is only because they have sacrificed their lives for the honor and glory of God—not because there is anything wrong with sexual intercourse."

She gave us the facts without batting an eye. She did turn a little red when, after she told us to scoot along over to church, she said she was going to offer her Holy Thursday communion for us girls and pray that each of us who chose the married state would grow up to make happy marriages.

All through the Holy Thursday Mass, instead of paying attention to the Washing of the Feet and the nine verses of the "Ubi Caritas" antiphon, I thought about the time when I'd be grown up and get to crawl under the covers with my husband. *My darling Aubrey, I love you with my whole heart, my whole mind, and my whole soul . . .* I daydreamed as Monsignor McGoffey intoned the "Pange lingua" off key.

The facts were new to Rosie, too. And she hated them. I found out on the way home from church.

"It's the most disgusting thing I've ever heard, it's filthy," she said furiously. She made a noise in her throat like throwing up.

"Can you imagine having to let Toomey or somebody do that to you? I'd throw up in his face." She made the gagging sound so loud a little kid stuck in a playpen in front of the house we were walking past started crying.

I said she probably wouldn't marry Toomey anyway.

"Well, I'm never doing it with anybody, ever."

"You gotta, if you want to have children," I said. I thought, but didn't say, my sister is going to do it.

"When you have babies," Rosie said, "it's a mess and you scream your head off."

I thought of my mother's bad back. We were bringing her

home from the hospital that afternoon. She'd warned us that she'd be wearing a big ugly brace under her dress.

Then Rosie asked me what I thought of the facts. I said they sounded okay, I wouldn't mind doing it if I really liked the other person.

"You must be crazy," she said.

We had come to the lot where we'd smoked our first cigarettes. We stood on the sidewalk peeling birch bark off two different trees. Rosie looked at me, as if she wanted to start a fight. "I'm gonna be a nun anyway, so there's nothin' to worry about."

Back in the fourth grade we both wanted to be nuns, but only during the Sacred Heart Novena in June. This time, Rosie sounded dead serious.

We never talked about boys or the facts again. Holy Saturday afternoon I brought the flowers from our garden over to her apartment to make Easter corsages for our mothers. The tulips and irises were out and the first azaleas were budding like baby candle flames. We had to whisper because Rosie's father was sleeping in the next room. He worked nights fixing trains at Penn Station. "Quirk ditched me last night for Monica Sheridan," I whispered. "She had another party—a private one, on Good Friday—and didn't invite us on purpose. Toomey was there, too." "Who cares?" Rosie whispered back. I wished I could be like her and not care. I was burning up from humiliation and hate. To change the subject, I whispered that I'd started reading *The Diary of Anne Frank.* "You ain't allowed to read that," Rosie said, not whispering anymore. She'd finished her mother's corsage and was working

on the six small ones for her sisters. "Says who?" I said, in a
normal tone of voice. "Sister Richard Dolores said it was a
fraud—you heard her." Dicky Dee had said no thirteen-year-
old girl could possibly have written it and recommended that
we not order it, even though it was offered by the Scholastic
Magazine Book Club our class belonged to. "Dicky Dee
doesn't know everything," I said. "You think *you* know more
than she does?" The way she said it, you'd never dream we
were friends. I raised my voice a little. "Eleanor Roosevelt
says Anne Frank wrote it and she wrote the preface." "Oh,
God, that ugly old pig," Rosie almost shouted, tying the last
perfect pink bow on her sisters' corsages. Then her mother
came out of the kitchen and told Rosie if she woke up her
father she'd catch it. I knew she meant it was time for me to
go home, so I did.

Rosie was the only school friend I invited to Irene's wedding that summer. And I told her some strictly confidential
stuff about Irene's husband-to-be not being able to stand our
family and how Irene had never had many dates, but here she
was getting married practically right out of high school and my
mother and father had ranted and raved and Irene had cried
since the day she and Steve got engaged. Rosie didn't say it,
but I knew she was thinking that if Irene was crazy enough to
get married she deserved to be miserable. She came to the
wedding, though. She even wore a dress.

Not long after Irene and Steve's wedding, Rosie's mother
had the baby boy the O'Gradys had wanted for a long time.
They moved into a house then, on the same side of Northern
Boulevard we lived on. But though Rosie and I now lived

closer to each other, we got together less and less. She sort of
went into hiding in her new house. Instead of chasing boys in
Bowne Park in the afternoons, she stayed home and practiced
the accordion in her new back yard. She got fat. Only once
before we graduated from St. Francis Assisi school was it ever
like old times again. Together, over the Easter vacation when
we were two months shy of our diplomas, we sold two hundred chance books—one hundred books, or 2,500 chances
each—on a 1954 four-door Buick sedan. The other fifty-three
kids in the 8B class sold the required four books each, except
for Gregory Burke who always turned up with forty books.
His father was bartender at the Blue Note where he palmed
off chances with every round on the men of the parish who
jammed the place on Monday nights after the meeting of the
Holy Name Society. Rosie and I were jealous of Pimple
Burke's title as SFA's Most Cooperative Chance Book Vendor
and we had nothing but contempt for the sissy way he won it.
We vowed to win the title from him once before graduating.
We wanted also to impress the 8B teacher, whom we both
adored, with our school spirit. But, most of all I aimed at
selling one hundred books because I respected that number.
I connected one hundred with total energy and effort and
success: I felt good only when I got 100 percent on a test; my
sister Irene wanted to die at fifty, but I didn't plan on giving
in before I was one hundred; I planned to someday walk or
bicycle one hundred miles.

I might have lived up to that last ambition in the course of
breaking Pimple Burke's record. Most parishioners bought
their chance books through the mail and a few days into the
Spring Chance Book Drive nonparishioners stopped answer-

ing their doorbells, they got so sick of kids from St. Francis'
getting them out of bed or off the john to chant "Would juh
like to buy a twenty-five cent chance on a nineteen fifty-four
four-door Buick sedan?" The few buyers we might uncover
within the parish limits weren't worth the time it would take
to find them, so on Easter Monday we struck out for fresh
territory. For the next six days we left Flushing on our bikes
every morning at nine and headed east on Northern Boulevard, pedaling chances in every store and bar and car lot along
the way. I got home before dark and counted and hid that
day's haul under the bed in a Ritz crackers box. We had great
luck. The seams of the first box split on Tuesday.

The bars were the best places and the daytime drunks the
easiest customers. They didn't act like they were doing us a big
favor by taking a lousy twenty-five cent chance. Most people
said, "Well, I usually buy from our own children, but I guess
I can help you out, too." (They meant St. Kevin's kids in
Bayside, St. Anastasia's in Douglaston, Snows in Floral Park,
St. Mary's in Manhasset. I don't know what parish Great Neck
was in, but I named it St. Patricia Murphy's after its Patricia
Murphy's Candlelight Restaurant—that place looked just like
a Long Island church with its packed parking lot and ladies in
mink stoles.) The drunks didn't cluck over our having come
out from Flushing either. The farther east we got on Northern
Boulevard or Route 25A, the bigger the fuss from car sales-
men and real estate agents over how "far" we had come. (In
1917 my father used to bike on Sunday mornings from Kew
Gardens to Babylon along Sunrise Highway and get back in
time for lunch.) And the drunks were the only ones who liked
our looks. After the long uphill stretch between Bayside and

Douglaston, Rosie tied the arms of her red windbreaker around her waist. The climb made my cheeks flaming red and my hair flew all over the place in the April wind. The ladies in Loretta's or Lisa's or Lynn's Beauty Parlor bought our chances because they felt sorry for us or thought we were orphans. "Does your *mother* know you're way out here?" But our jeans and old jackets put us over with the bums and the bartenders who never stopped us from selling to their customers. Patricia Murphy's and Howard Johnson's threw us out every time.

The only hard part was getting home before my mother got suspicious. I'd told her I was spending Easter vacation studying for Regents at Rosie's. Back in the fourth grade when I was selling chances in Flushing, a teen-age boy on a black English racer had tried to molest me late one November afternoon. Ever since then my mother had forbidden me to sell chances even on our own block. The day we hit Port Washington at three o'clock, having come top speed along Old Country Road, and then had to race back to Flushing before making the trip at all worthwhile—I hated being forced to waste my time like that. Having to sacrifice the homecoming crowds I knew would pour from the Long Island Railroad stations in another hour—and buy our chances while they waited for their wives and chauffeurs—it made me furious to have to pass up all those rich businessmen. And every day tempting road signs made me think how great it would be to keep riding east and the hell with fooling my mother anymore or selling chances. The names "Northport," "Riverhead," and "Orient Point" I remembered as magic places where we used to swim and dig for clams and get corn and tomatoes when I was small. To go there under my own steam and explore . . . to keep going . . . As I grew able to ride rather than walk up 25A's long hills, I became cocksure that I could make it out there. The desire to reach the tip of Long Island was the first passion of my life.

I always beat my mother home before six and got my legs back by running up and down stairs two at a time. The lying made the 25A adventure all the more exciting. While helping her peel the vegetables, I thought of the day's journey, how the wind had felt, the uphill panting and downhill fear, the all-day motion of pushing and pedaling and steering and selling and rushing against time. I did not enjoy thinking of the explosion I knew would take place if she found out what I was up to. If my run-in with the Flushing sex maniac hadn't been enough to turn her against the chance-book drive forever, she had since heard the nuns' stories about little children selling chance books who had been found in apartment house incinerators, chopped up into little pieces by crazies. She didn't understand that the stories were meant to teach the importance of always being in the state of grace—one knows not the place or the hour—not the dangers of chance-book selling. And she didn't realize that if you didn't sell the required four books, you came close to having your head cut off. Delinquent girls got double homework for a week, but the boys . . . we nicknamed one nun Sister Krazy Kellogg for her Snap-Crackle-and-Pop techniques. For her Whacko-Smacko-and-Kill-'em methods, Rosie had dubbed Sister Jane Agnes the Agony.

She had scourged us through 8A, which we endured by hating her and by looking forward to the 8B room where reigned Sister Mary, the most popular teacher in the school.

It is impossible to describe the rage I felt and that I saw come over Rosie's face when we filed into our 8B classroom the Monday morning after vacation—Rosie and I bearing eight Ritz cracker boxes stuffed with money and stubs—and found not our fabulous Sister Mary but Sister Jane Agnes instead.

"Sister Mary has been taken ill and will be in Immaculata Hospital until June at least. I will get you through the Regents and graduation. Sister Mary Thecla has taken over my 8A duties."

It was the Agony herself who had dreamed up the school-wide chance-book drive ten years before. Each of the sixteen classes named itself after a football or baseball team and there were eight contests every morning between the sixteen "teams." The Principal reported the final scores over the public address system.

"Notre Dame [Grade 7A] versus Fordham [Grade 4B]: Notre Dame, seventy dollars."

Seven A dug its nails in, held its breath, their teacher held the crucifix on her rosary tight.

"Fordham, eighty-one dollars."

Out of the public address box blared the screaming and stamping of the hysterical, victorious Grade 4B.

Rosie and I stacked our cracker boxes on the Agony's desk and told her our totals.

"Well, well." That was all she said about our feat. No one in the history of the school had ever sold one hundred chance books before.

She fancied herself the school's expert at playing the chance-book game, but during the next half hour she collapsed. Her special strategy had been handing in an unusual amount like $101 for any one game, figuring the rival team would hand in $100 or some even, predictable number. Her other trick was to hold back some money from Monday's game and use it as a reserve with which to boost our totals toward the end of the week when the selling spirit of the teams had fallen off. On this Monday morning, her two tricks having worked for ten years, Sister Jane Agnes tried them again: she handed in $101 and held back Rosie's and my $1,250. But the teacher of the team we were playing had been around long enough to catch on to the Agony's favorite play. She turned in $102 and our class lost the game by one stinking dollar.

Then the Agony went berserk. She blamed us. Kicking the wastepaper basket off her platform, she screamed that we weren't going to get away with humiliating her like this, she would make us pay. For a starter, she refused to teach us. We could flunk the Regents and it would serve us right. "Take out your arithmetic books. Start the problems on page ninety and when I think you've learned a lesson, I'll tell you." She sat down at Sister Mary's desk, looking as mean as Captain Bligh.

We thought she'd call a halt after lunch but she only snapped, "Continue." If you looked up from your desk, her eyes caught yours immediately and riddled them; if you looked sideways or turned around, you risked becoming the first girl to get hit—she looked that mean. She sat up there as if she had a bull whip in the drawer ready to land on the first one who squawked. There seemed nothing to do but sit there and do the arithmetic problems, stinging with hatred.

On Wednesday morning I looked up from page 150 of the

arithmetic book and caught her staring out the window at the spring sky and suddenly smile. She'll give in today, I guessed. But she didn't. At three o'clock we wound up our third day of silence, arithmetic, and sitting. No one could leave to go to the bathroom, since if you raised your hand to ask she ignored you. She ignored us so completely that Big Toomey got away with drawing fat ladies on the underside of his arms in ballpoint and making them gyrate by clenching and unclenching his fists. Joe Kessner cracked up the whole back of the room one day by opening his belt and slowly unbuttoning his tan uniform shirt and pulling out five Archie comics, which he then read so intently he dribbled on his desk and the gum dropped out of his mouth. On the fourth day, Fat Fox, who was so big the drugstores sold him cigarettes without asking his age, ate three pages out of his arithmetic book and then chewed up his pencil till only the lead and metal tip around the eraser were left.

On Friday morning I noticed how red in the face the Agony got when we did not scream or even clap when the principal announced Steubenville, the name of our class's team—and of Sister Mary's hometown—had trampled St. Peter's. We hadn't clapped or screamed for any of the victories Rosie's and my haul had brought us that week. I saw now that our silence, broadcast to the whole school, had been infuriating her all week.

That afternoon I walked home from school with Robert Quinn, a tall boy who lived across the street from me, and we joked about starting a revolt. The next day I ran into him after Confession, and we began to organize. By Sunday the word got around and most of the class met in Bowne Park that afternoon. We ran through the strategy; 8B went wild with anticipation.

"At nine A.M. we'll all blow our noses," I shouted.

"At nine-fifteen we will all run our thumbnails along the teeth of our pocket combs," roared Quinn.

"At nine-thirty everyone drop their rulers."

"At nine forty-five we all bend down and untie and then re-tie our shoelaces. If you don't have shoelaces on your shoes, just count to ten instead."

Our spirit was as strong as the sails on the children's boats whipping across the lake. The class cheered each of the twelve operations we'd planned for every fifteen minutes until twelve o'clock when Jane Agnes, realizing she was licked, would be forced to end her reign of terror. After all, what could she do. She couldn't beat up all fifty-four of us, we told one another. Fat Fox, who had watched the briefing from the high branch of a tree where he sat blowing smoke rings, shouted down that he would be happy to set the classroom on fire if the revolt failed. When Spike Sponsella moved we adjourn to Cy's Drugs for Pigs' Dinners on the house, Fat Fox jumped from the tree, swung Spike up on his shoulders, and led the parade out of the park. (Spike's father was Cy, the druggist who kept the convent in Dixie cups on all major feast days.)

But the next day it was all over by ten o'clock. Between 9:45 and 10:00 A.M. I watched Jane Agnes whip the most loud-mouthed rebels into a pack of cringing pups. It happened so fast it's hard to know just what made us fall so easily.

She was purple and quivering by 9:45 when we got down on the floor for Operation Shoelaces. Operations Nose-blow,

Comb, and Ruler had gone off perfectly. After I untied and
tied my saddles once, I remember looking around and seeing
that everyone else was still huddled over their shoes. So I
decided to untie and tie my laces again, partly because I was
afraid to be the first one to sit up and have to feel her eyes and
partly because I got carried away. I wanted to make each part
of the Revolt last as long as possible. I guess I thought that
when the other kids saw I was still down they'd stay down too.
In fact, I thought, wouldn't it be a great operation if we all
crouched under our desks for a full fifteen minutes? If only I'd
thought of that one yesterday. It would be more fun than all
our tactics put together, we could even play cards or pretend
we were asleep. Oh, God, we could all snore! I started to look
around again to see if most people were ready to sit up.
Blocking my forward line of vision was a wall of brown skirt.

"All right, Miss Girlinghausen, you may sit up now. Your
little show is over."

She then got most of the kids to confess their part in the
"disrespectful display" and to name the ringleaders. "Anyone
who does not own up will be sorry. I am sure you all want to
graduate as much as we want to get rid of you." Like crazy
they confessed, ratted, and were pardoned. Robert Quinn, the
boy ringleader, got his head smashed against the wall a few
times, but he was big and didn't care and anyway on his tie
he wore a button saying "I Was A Pig At Cy's Drug" that
somehow made it seem as if he had laughed in her face.

She handled me the way you might treat a stranger who
vomited on you in a stuffy bus. I was told to move my desk
to the very back of the room, beyond where the fluorescent
lighting ended. *"Not* there. All the way back against the wall

over in the corner. As far away from us as you can go." I was to consider myself in exile until graduation. She waited until I was settled smack against the wall and there wasn't a sound. Then the final mopping up began.

"For an Eight-B class you are very immature. Your little games this morning were very silly. This childishness is not the way to make Sister Mary get well. I am disappointed in all of you, but it is still my duty to guide you. . . . There is nothing so disgusting as a tough girl. A boy who cuts up here and there we can understand; we expect it. But all I can tell you about a girl who is an upstart, who is *fresh* . . . is stay away from her. She will never be any good. She is nothing but a disgrace to her family and her school and most of all to God. If you follow Miss Girlinghausen's example, you will be sorry. May I remind you that your catechism names bad companions as one major occasion of sin?" (She paused and turned to look straight at Rosie.) "This morning Miss Girlinghausen made a fool of herself and by following her you did too. I am surprised at some of you. You may be impressed by her grades, but the road to hell is filled with people who use their God-given talents for evil. Her high marks mean absolutely nothing in the eyes of God. I order you to have nothing further to do with her while you are in this classroom. If she asks to borrow as much as a scrap of paper, do not answer her, do not let on you know she is in this room. Think of her as invisible. I hope she will use this opportunity to think about where she is headed. Nobody wants a fresh girl."

I sat back in my dim corner and tried to look cool. But I felt like a freak of nature.

Then she announced it was time to get started on the Regents review and she had the class on her side for the rest of the term. A lot of the boys, especially, thought the June break depended on the Agony torturing them with her famous daily Regents drill. "In all my years of preparing graduates for Regents, I have never had anyone fail, either English or Social Studies or Mathematics. Of course, this year there is Mr. Kessner back there." The ranks laughed and turned around to look at Joe Kessner who was supposed to be the dumbest kid ever to go through St. Francis. And I knew she had won them over completely when I tried to borrow a pencil from a few kids in the back of the room and they ignored me, even when she wasn't looking.

I thought of what my mother said when anybody gave her the frost—"Two can play that game." I decided to ignore the Agony right back, to make believe she was dead, did not exist at all. I realized that eight weeks of solitary confinement gave me an opportunity to concentrate so hard on my own private Regents review I could probably get 100 percent in all three of them. No one in the history of the school had ever graduated with an average of 100 percent. When Monsignor McGoffey announced my perfect score from the pulpit at the Graduates' Mass, the whole church would gasp and the Agony —along with her goons—would know I had done it all by myself. I knew from Irene and Nony that all you had to do to rack up on the Regents was memorize the questions and answers on the old ones and review the things you weren't perfectly sure of again and again. The afternoon of the Revolt I began memorizing: the dates of Manassas and Bunker Hill, the products made in the Finger Lakes' towns, the number of apples Mr. Banks lost if he dropped two-thirds of his original load of three thousand apples on his way to marketing them in Corning at two cents a piece and dribbled one-fourth of the remainder as he hurried to take shelter from a hurricane somewhere in the Genesee Valley. By the time the term had worn almost to its end I had become expert at spotting the questions that reappeared every year in different disguises—Mr. Banks of the lost apples of Corning became the next year Mr. Smith with ears of corn in Elmira.

Sometimes, when Sister Jane Agnes's back was turned and I saw people passing out invitations to graduation parties to just about everyone but me, I thought about crawling up to her desk at three o'clock and saying I was sorry about the Revolt. But I remembered what mother had said the time Nony, knowing she'd be thrown off her high school newspaper if she refused to sign a petition opposing the censure of Senator McCarthy, had asked her for advice. "This above all: to thine own self be true," mother told her. I stayed put in my unapologetic seat.

I rattled my cage only once, during a panel discussion on the topic "Why Senator McCarthy Is a Great American." Since the day of the Revolt, when Rosie had started boycotting our secret lunchtime smokes in the Myrtle Avenue lot, I had spent the time at home puffing her share of the Pall Malls and watching the Army–McCarthy hearings on television. At seven o'clock I watched them again while my parents shrieked curses at Sister Jane Agnes's hero and told me and Nony why

McCarthy was "The Most Dangerous Man in America." So while the Agony led the class in interrupting the panelists' speeches with applause, I sat back in my corner doodling swastikas and tearing my desk blotter. I tore and tore and tore, but I could not ignore them—the quotes from *The Tablet,* the panelists' nervous glances at Jane Agnes to see if she was pleased, the lies about Mother's and Daddy's heroes, Roosevelt and Stevenson and Joseph Welch.

"Senator McCarthy is not only a great American, he is a devout Catholic as well," Joanne Bishop was saying. "It is a well-known fact that he stops in to pay a visit in the Senate chapel and kneel before the Blessed Mother's altar as often as his busy schedule will permit. Where else do you think he slips off to so faithfully every morning during the hearings?"

"The john, stupid!" I shouted from the back of the room.

The class looked so scared, you'd think I'd shot a spitball at the crucifix. The Agony blanched. Then she sentenced me to stay after school till five o'clock for the rest of the term.

All through the long spring afternoons, then, I sat back in my stuffy corner while fat high school girls whom Sister Jane Agnes had taught in the eighth grade dropped into our 8B classroom for old times' sake. They draped themselves all over the Agony's desk, swapping gossip about her beloved junior senator. The Agony turned off the overhead lights at three o'clock so I couldn't read. Instead, I distracted myself with filth. I wrote in my notebook the worst curse words I knew.

"In our history classes at Cardinal McGinty, the assignment for the rest of the term is to listen to Fulton Lewis every night, and last night our whole family listened together," one pasty-faced creep volunteered earnestly.

"Dumb Bitch," I wrote, leaning heavily on the pencil.

"*My* history teacher says McCarthy has a lifetime subscription to *The Tablet,*" one of the frumps said sanctimoniously.

"Shut Up Shithead," I scrawled over and over.

And whenever I compared what it used to feel like riding my bike on soft May afternoons through Alley Pond Park with what it felt like sitting all afternoon in the Agony's airless box, or whenever I remembered my mother's questions about when the graduation parties were going to start, I went all the way. I printed in huge dark capital letters, "FUCK YOU, Sister Jane Agnes." It was the dirtiest and most forbidden expression I knew. Most of my friends said plenty of "craps" and "damns," but none of the girls said "fuck." Ever. I didn't know what it meant, I had never said it out loud, and I thought myself terribly daring to put it in writing. I unloaded my foul heart letter by letter, upper and lower case, forward and backward—"Senga Enaj Retsis Uoy Kcuf."

Once I would have shown my dirty work to Rosie and she would have added a few curses of her own. But lately she'd been volunteering to decorate the Agony's bulletin boards for her. I thought Rosie might rat on me. The day I told her I'd gotten into the high school I'd wanted to go to, one smack in the middle of the city, she said, "I'm glad I won't have to travel to the *city,*" as if she felt sorry for me, as if she'd never planned to go to a city school herself, as if she was fifty years old.

For the Graduation Mass I bought my first bra, in Wool-
worth's, a size 30 AA. I hiked the straps up as far as they'd go
and stuffed the cups with the tissue paper from my new shoes.
My chest itched terribly all through the ceremony. The girl
graduates sat on the right side of the church. We fussed so
much with our high-heeled T-straps and curled hairdos blowing to bits under the tall altar fans that you could hear the pews
and kneelers creaking till the Agony came forward with the
Hairy Eyeball. After the Last Gospel, an altar boy unplugged
the fans as Monsignor McGoffey mounted the steps of the
pulpit. I began to chew my thumbnails much more viciously
than I had during all three Regents. If I didn't get 100, if I
didn't at least get the highest average in the class . . . I had to
have *something* to show for all that torture . . . If the Agony
had had my name taken off the Honor Roll, even though I did
make it . . . If my name was not called out at all . . .

By the time Monsignor had finished congratulating the class
and reading out the notices in the parish bulletin, my thumbs
were so sore and I was so stiff with fear of the worst that I felt
only physical relief when he finally announced, "In the New
York State Regents Examinations, the following graduates
have attained an average of ninety percent or higher: Martha
Anne Girlinghausen. Ninety-nine percent." As I stood for my
moment of glory, both bra straps broke at once. My underwear was as relieved as I was that though I hadn't gotten 100,
I'd gotten the highest, my name had been called out and called

out first, and I had done it on my own.

But the roll call wasn't over yet. After calling out the names on the Honor Roll, Monsignor paused and then in a creepy voice, said, "Following Our Saviour's example at the Marriage Feast of Cana, I have saved the best for last." The Honor Roll was long, he said, and the graduates whose names appeared on it had brought honor to the parish and their families. But our success, he said, was as nothing compared to the honor it was now his privilege to announce.

"History has been made in this year of Our Lord, nineteen fifty-four. Never before has the parish of St. Francis Assisi been blessed with a vocation to the Sisterhood among those so young as our dear grammar school graduates you see before you today." Then he said that Rose Mary O'Grady—*Rosie*— would leave for the Franciscan Juniorate of Our Lady of the Woods in Columbus, Ohio, in just one week's time. After a lot of blah-blah-blah about her wonderful Catholic parents and her teachers, the good sisters, the organist blasted the first bars of "Pomp and Circumstance" loud enough to shake the choir loft down from the walls. We marched out of church two-by-two to his stupid *fortissimo.* My tissue paper falsies fell out from under my gown as the Agony clapped her hands and the graduates turned about face and genuflected toward the high altar.

Out in the school yard, which was packed with graduates and their families, I stood near the Blessed Mother's grotto and waited for some space to open up before trying to thread my way through the crowd over to my family. In a small clearing in the center of the yard a photographer was posing Rosie and her family with Monsignor McGoffey. Rosie's mother and father were smiling all over themselves like sunbaths. Mr. O'Grady held the baby boy on his shoulders.

Then I watched Monsignor make his way over to where my family was standing waiting for me, Mother and Daddy, Grandma and Grandpa Sullivan, Nony, Steve, and Irene, who was expecting her first baby any day. I could hear Mother's voice above the crowd, exclaiming about my 99, as they shook hands all around.

And then along came the Agony. She kissed Nony, whom she had also taught and whom she liked, hugged my mother, shook hands with my father, and kept her distance from Irene, which was good luck for the baby.

By this time it would have been easy for me to push through the crowd to my family. But I stayed where I was and watched. Sister Jane Agnes was beaming at everyone, as if she was in love with the world. A lot of people stopped to shake her hand and she introduced them all to the family of the girl who had gotten the highest average in the history of the parish. They all looked thrilled to the gills with one another. I didn't blame my parents really. They knew nothing about the Revolt—telling them would have meant letting it out about selling one hundred chance books on Long Island and that would have been the end of my bike. But I did not see why they had to fall all over Jane Agnes, let her flatter them, when they did not like her politics and had known she was a lousy teacher when Nony had had her.

Then, from my spot behind the grotto, I heard the Agony say, "Martha is certainly a feather in all our caps today!"

I ducked down behind the hydrangea bushes and made it around the convent to the side door of the school without being seen. I returned my cap and gown to my old classroom and went to wait for my family in the car. When they finally came along wondering what on earth can be keeping that child, I'd pretend I'd felt sick.

I had—at the thought that within their jolly circle the Agony might have tried to shake my hand or put her arm around me. That I would have had to smile and pretend that I didn't hate her, that I was a genius instead of just a good memorizer, that I thought it was good news that Rosie was taking off. Hiding in the car, I felt like a bandit who had made a good getaway. I was going to a high school in the city, where no one knew me, where I'd meet people from places like Brooklyn and Manhattan. The noon Angelus began to ring as Irene and Steve came walking slowly up the block toward the car. I'd never have to lay eyes on the Agony's ugly puss again. I was finished with St. Francis Assisi School at last, forever and ever, world without end. Amen.

3

There's no such thing as starting over. That summer Mary-mound Academy for Young Ladies at 46 East 68th Street got for its head warden Fat Josie from Jersey City. She had punctured Eugene Kessner's eardrums when Irene had her in the sixth grade at St. Francis Assisi. When I picked a high school run by her order—the same one that staffed St. Francis—Irene warned me Josie might turn up again. But the spring before I started high school, she was safely teaching typing at All Martyrs and anyway Marymound Academy was supposed to be a classy school, the order's showplace. They'd never let a fishwife like Josie get her foot inside the Servants' Entrance.

Instead they put her in the Principal's Office. She lumbered out to call the roll of the Freshman class our first day of school.

"Maria Mannion. Mary Donoghue. Margaret Murphy. That's a good Irish name, Margaret. I taught your brother John at All Martyrs. Nina I . . . I-io- . . . I-on-dola? Another good Irish name, get that hair back off your face. Martha

Girlinghosen. I had your sister in Flushing. Wipe that smile off your face. Mary Anne O'Connor. You're the scholarship from Saint Joan's. We'll be watching you."

We were lined up in the ballroom. I touched the velvet-covered wall and glanced up at a twelve-foot high portrait of a woman in a white gown with a plunging neckline. Josie had been the only nun at St. Francis who hit girls.

The Mother General at the order's Motherhouse must have been plastered the day she put an animal like Josie in charge of a place like the Academy. Originally the building had been the residence of Colonel Joseph Friedman, a rich Jewish man whose best friend was a Catholic. On his deathbed, according to the nuns, Colonel Friedman gave the house to his Catholic friend, Mr. Kirk, who was also Cardinal Spellman's best friend, according to the nuns. Mr. Kirk gave the mansion to his favorite nuns, the Franciscan Sisters of Our Lady of the Woods. They turned it into a school for two hundred girls, but except for adding desks, chalkboards, and pictures of the Sacred Heart, they weren't allowed to make any big changes. Mr. Kirk wanted the mansion always to look the way it had when the Colonel lived there.

The first day of school we came through a glass front door encased in iron filigree. (After that, everyone except the priests had to use the Servants' Entrance.) The front lobby, which was loaded with carved oak tables and chairs the Colonel had picked up in England, led to a long white marble staircase. A red carpet ran up the middle of it to the second floor and stopped at the threshold of the chapel, which in the yearbook was called "the heart of the school." It had sliding wood doors with carved panels full of prophets and saints having visions. The interior of the chapel smelled of floor wax.

On the next three floors were the classrooms where Colonel Friedman's fortune lived on in the crystal chandeliers, French doors, and huge walk-in fireplaces with mirrors dripping gilty curlicues over the mantels. Along the corridor outside the library were stained-glass windows with scenes from *The Divine Comedy* that he had brought back from Europe. As we filed down a narrow hall to our classroom, some upperclassmen glided out of a coat room and tiptoed around our line, smiling like cover girls. Their hairdos were out of a magazine, the shine on their brown shoes matched the mahogany woodwork, the pleats in their uniform skirts were pressed in like razor blades. Just before we got to our home room we passed a bathroom with a huge marble sink and brass faucets shaped like lions' heads. A nun was standing in the doorway watching some girls who were primping and laughing. From the way she smiled at them and then said, "Vanity, thy name is woman" you could tell she admired them as much as they admired themselves. That first morning, even the nuns looked ladylike. Like rich women touring a museum, they moved through the halls, smiling remotely, never looking at anyone they passed.

The Freshman teachers were so old they couldn't talk above a whisper. Only one was able to stay on her feet and write on the board while she taught. The Religion teacher fell asleep and dribbled down the bib of her habit the first day of classes. The History nun told us five times in forty-five minutes that she had to keep pills under her pillow in case she had another heart attack in the middle of the night. The rest of the time she warned us about Hunter College. It was only half a block

away from our school, just across Park Avenue. She said it was
no accident that they built it right across the street from the
Russian Consulate because it was a hotbed of Communists and
should be painted pink. She prayed every morning that the
Marymound girls would make the walk from the Lexington
Avenue subway to the Academy safe from the snares of the
enemy.

The only one who still had her marbles was Sister Cecilia,
the old Principal from St. Francis Assisi. She'd been trans-
ferred to the Academy to teach Latin. She had gotten a bit
hunchbacked, but every morning she introduced us to the
declensions with eagerness, as if they were dear old friends she
could hardly wait to have us meet.

When Sister Cecilia passed you in the halls, she didn't look
straight ahead as if you were part of the wall. She looked you
in the eye and said, "Good morning, Martha," or Mary, or
whoever you were. She knew all our names by the end of the
first week, and as the school librarian, she seemed to know the
titles of every book in the library. The books were her family:
she knew the good ones and the bad ones by heart, and she
liked some and hated others. The first time I went in to look
for a book, she showed me around the different sections of the
library as if it were her home. At the end of the tour she
stopped in front of the fireplace carved with small stone heads
of laughing angels. "There's a lot of rubbish here, Martha,"
she said. "Gifts from alumnae and benefactors and the like.

But there are fine things, too, and if you read enough, you'll find out the difference for yourself."

After a few weeks of classes it was plain that the only thing special about the Academy was its location. Only one person, an Italian girl, seemed brilliant, and quite a few students, it turned out, had failed the entrance exam. They had gotten into Marymound on the pull of their big-shot uncles in the Chancery. Except for a few from Manhattan, most of the girls came from the same ordinary places as Nony's friends at Mary Immaculate High School in Queens—Woodside, Jackson Heights, Flushing itself. And for all my daily traveling companions seemed to realize, we might as well have been going to school in Steubenville, Ohio. Every morning we met on the last car of the Main Street–Times Square eight o'clock Super Express. At the Plaza we changed to the BMT and from there the ride was underground. All we saw of the live city, day in and day out, was the block and a half between the Lexington Avenue subway stop and the Servants' Entrance of school. Morning and afternoon, it was the Foundling, Hunter High School, Hunter College, Dr. Neufeld, D.D.S., the Russian Consulate, Park Avenue poodles, and finally Fat Josie peeking out from the school doorway to see if the *Journal-American* had been delivered yet and if she could catch one of us not wearing the uniform hat.

One afternoon in October I suggested we go for a soda on Third Avenue before getting the train back to Flushing. You'd think I'd said let's strip and swim the East River. Patricia Cleary from Little Neck said immediately that that was against the rules we were supposed to have memorized in the school handbook. We could get expelled for "loitering in local establishments" after school in uniform.

We were standing on the traffic island in Park Avenue, waiting for a green light. I looked at Cleary, pure beef-to-the-heels, and at the rest of my white-gloved, uniform-hatted companions, all headed, as usual, straight for home. Don't wait, I mumbled, I just remembered . . . my Latin book, and I turned around and walked against the light, in front of the southbound taxis, and then west toward Fifth Avenue. I had no specific destination in mind, simply the determination not to waste time in an overgrown Girl Scout troop anymore.

I was walking so fast I would have passed him by if he hadn't suddenly stopped to bend down and tie his shoelace on the sidewalk of Grand Army Plaza. I tripped over him—Robert Quinn, the boy ringleader of the eighth grade Revolt. He now went to Regis on Eighty-something Street. We walked down to the Forty-second Street library together. After we applied for cards, I went outside and waited for him on the steps. I stared at the stone lions lording it over Fifth Avenue. They looked sure and strong, like gods who were keeping watch before the temple of the queen of cities. New York the Lionhearted, I thought, as I watched Quinn coming down the wide white steps. He looked fabulous in the city, not like an ordinary boy from Flushing. In Bryant Park we ate pretzels and he sounded as determined as I was to see, touch, taste, cross, walk, smell, every inch of New York while we had the chance. Who knows what Podunk we'll be stuck in four years from now, I said. "*I* will never leave this city," Quinn said solemnly, as if he were making a vow.

On silver-gold Sundays we began to explore. The Brooklyn Botanical Gardens, Riverside Park, Marble Hill. We walked across the George Washington Bridge, followed the Hudson up along the Palisades, jostled in and out of the monkey houses at the Bronx Zoo. Most places we were discovering for the first time so we were equals, more like friends than dates. He liked the Frick best because it had Holbein's painting of St. Thomas More, who Quinn said was his ideal man. Because it was the strangest, my favorite of all the places we went that fall was the Cloisters. It's a museum that looks like a monastery, sitting high on a bluff overlooking the Hudson, and to the south, the great gray bridge. Inside, we looked at the Unicorn tapestries, the weird carvings on the Romanesque arches, the mysterious face of the madonna in the Langon chapel—every part of the place seemed to send off magnetic waves and I couldn't stop staring. Outside, at the end of a rampart walk, Quinn pinned his class pin on my sweater. It was a raw November afternoon, and we were the only people on the promontory. He kissed me. My back was to the river. Over his shoulder I saw the gold-leaved trees in Fort Tryon Park, shivering.

A class pin or a boy's ring was supposed to turn your life into a little blue heaven. It didn't even give me the nerve to call Quinn by his first name. Back in grammar school, everyone went by last names. Now, if I called Quinn "Bob" to his face, I'd be admitting I liked him, that he was more than just another old friend from St. Francis. But I couldn't keep calling him "Quinn." "What is wrong with 'Robert'?" my mother asked. "That *is* the boy's name, after all." "Call him 'Freckles,' " Nony said, trying to cut him down to size. (She thought he was precocious because he made fun of the Legion of Decency and had seen *The Moon Is Blue.*) The night of the

Turkey Trot, Regis High School's Thanksgiving Dance, I found out his full name, and for a little while, my problem was solved.

Because she didn't know about the walk to the Rodeo, my mother insisted that the Turkey Trot was Martha's First Date. She made me and Quinn pose for the camera as if we were a *Saturday Evening Post* cover, Quinn in his good blue suit, me with a corsage on a new dress and suffocating to death in the brassalette I wore underneath. On the way into the city it dug into my baby fat so hard I thought I was bleeding from the armpits. Right after the first dance I went to the ladies' room, took out the steels, and jammed them into my mother's tiny evening bag.

Quinn was president of his class and he said socializing was part of his job. When he spotted yet another priest standing near the punch bowl whom he said he should say hello to, I asked him if this one was the janitor or somebody big. This one, Quinn said, was the Prefect of Discipline. The priests who stood around the edge of the dance floor were like a pack of watchdogs. This one was their leader. Just as were walking over to him, the band started playing "Take the 'A' Train," which was the best number they'd done all night. We were missing "The 'A' Train" for the Prefect of Discipline.

Quinn introduced me. The Prefect cupped his ear and said, "What's the name? Give it to me slowly now."

Here we go again, I thought. The "G-i-r-l-i-n-g-h-a-u-s-e-n? What kind of a name is that?" bit.

I cut Quinn off. "Thertainly, Father," I lisped, slowly. My name ith Martha Thuh—Thuh—*Thullivan.*"

Quinn knuckled me in the back and the priest hesitated.

Then, very proud of himself, he said, "Oh! *Sullivan!* And where are you from, Miss Sullivan?"

"Thuh-Thunny-thide."

"Ah, *Sunny*side!" "The 'A' Train" was now at full volume. It was great music.

"And do you go to school in Sunnyside, Miss Sullivan?"

I leaned toward him and stared at his lips, squinting. "Yeth."

He lit his pipe as the band dragged out the final chord of "The 'A' Train" and gazed out at the dance floor, probably looking for couples in need of his discipline. "The 'A' Train" was over. To get rid of us he said, "Well, that's fine now. Isn't that the Bunny Hop they're lining up for? Why don't you two join the fun?"

We left the dance then because Quinn said I belonged in a cage. As class president, he said, he had his reputation to protect. He was kidding—how could the leader of the Revolt against the Agony give a damn about a Prefect of Discipline?

From the Turkey Trot we went to the Rainbow, a bar in Yorkville that was off limits for Regis students, and was therefore, Quinn said, their favorite hangout. When the waiter asked our ages, we said eighteen without blinking. (I could handle liquor because every month my mother gave me Tom Collinses for cramps—she said nothing did the trick like gin.) After a few rounds at the Rainbow, we went across Eighty-sixth Street to the Hofbrau House, which Quinn said had good singing. He knew the words to every song. At the end of "Muss I Denn," a German song we played on the piano for my father to sing, he knocked his stein against mine at the words "Mein Schatz." They mean "My dear."

When Fritz the waiter spilled beer on a girl at our table, I
opened my bag for a Kleenex. As if I'd used a slingshot, the
steels from my brassalette shot out of the bag. They whizzed
through the air, over heads and tables, and ricocheted against
the Schnitzelbank screen and off the stage, plinging like man-
dolin strings tuned too tight. Some people laughed and looked
around, but they hadn't seen which table the fusillade had
come from. But Quinn had.

He broke up. "So that's what you did with your underwear.
What do you call them? Bones?"

I tried to look as if he was just too immature. "What *are* you
talking about?"

"Oh, c'mon," he said, and then he reached around and
squeezed my waist, tickling me. "That suit of armor you had
on. Even if I hadn't felt the difference, I would have noticed."

"Really, you must be drunk," I said prissily. He still had his
hand on my hip.

"You are a little, uh, round, Martha, but you don't need
armor." He reached for a dry napkin and then he drew a
sketch of my body that made me look plump but in that
beautiful way, like the women in the paintings at the Frick. I
realized by drawing me naked he was taking liberties. *"If
liberties are taken, liberties are lost,"* Mother said. I realized his
being so frank might mean he did not respect me. But his
sketch was good, just like his singing. And what he said about
the underwear was true. So I went to collect my shrapnel—
I'd get killed if I came home without the guts of the contrap-
tion, which cost $8.99 in Mays.

When I came back to the table, Quinn was still making
sketches of naked women. He told me that when he was a little

boy he'd drawn a whole bunch of nudes in a notebook. "When my mother found it, she went nuts," he said. I could see he was getting slightly smashed because he rambled on asking me if my ancestors were Dutch or German or what and about how beautiful curves were and how he hadn't known what to say about the Nudie Notebook in confession, he was only nine, and didn't understand what was wrong with it. "Not that there was anything wrong." He downed half a stein in one swig.

We walked from Eighty-sixth Street to the Fifty-ninth Street Bridge, where we got a cab for Queens. On the way home Quinn sang one Irish folk song after another, good ones I'd never heard before—"The Wild Colonial Boy" and "Finnegan's Wake"—not the "Too-ra-loo-ra-loo-ra" gush we sang in assembly on St. Patrick's Day. He cracked up laughing halfway through one called "Bold Robert Emmet." He told me that whenever his Aunt Catherine got drunk she spread her legs apart and through her tears sang that song about Robert Emmet, the Irish patriot who led a suicidal attack on the British troops in Dublin Castle. In a maudlin voice he imitated his Aunt Catherine and sang:

> *The bold Robert Emmet, the darlin' of Erin,*
> *The bold Robert Emmet, he died with a smile.*
> *Farewell, companions both loyal and darin',*
> *I lay down my life for the emerald isle.*

"A typical Irish hero," he said. "He thought death was better than life. Do you know she actually made my mother name me after him? He's a family hero."

"Bold Robert Emmet? That's your full name?"

"Not Bold—just the other two. Robert Emmet. Quinn."

"Oh, I don't care, I've got it. From this day forward, I shall call you Bold Robert Emmet . . ."

"It's about time you called me something," he said.

The cab was barreling over Flushing Bridge and up Northern Boulevard as he started taking lovely liberties. He put his arm around me and I knew he could feel the roll of flab that bulged over the waist of my panty girdle.

Not long after that, Bold Robert Emmet disappeared. His mother, while cleaning his room over the Christmas holidays, discovered he was failing Greek. At Regis, which was a school for scholarship students only, they threw you out if you failed one subject, and the passing grade was 75. Robert spent the winter hibernating with Homer and Hector and Helen of Troy. He reappeared for the Regis spring boat ride to Bear Mountain. I'd been counting the days to our reunion, to coming home at night and watching the river from the top deck of the Hudson River Dayline, like Magnolia and Ravenal in *Show Boat.*

There was a good band on the boat, but we didn't dance because he said he didn't feel like it. The truth was he didn't feel like being seen dancing with me. I had gained a few pounds over the winter and I looked especially fat the day of the boat ride in my new full pink skirt. In the picture on the Simplicity pattern envelope, the hemline of the skirt looked like the petals of a tulip. I was the worst seamstress in the family: mine turned out looking like a dead tulip. To get the full-blown tulip effect, I'd worn my puffiest crinoline. Nony, after staying up half the night to fix the zipper which I'd put in upside down, tried to console me. "It isn't your style, Martha, but don't think about it—you have lovely hair, a perfect complexion, and the best neck in the family." But when he called for me that morning, Bold Robert looked at one thing only: *barrel ass* said his stare.

At Bear Mountain we went swimming, though it was freezing. The raw weather suited his mood. When we weren't having chicken fights with the only other couple from Regis in the pool, Quinn kept eyeing my blubber, which the rented tank suit—without skirt or ruffle—did not hide. ("That baby fat will drop off you like magic one of these days," my mother promised. "Nobody likes a skinny dame," my father lied.)

By the time we boarded the boat for home, my hair was so frizzy from the pool Robert said I looked like a carving we'd seen on an arch at the Cloisters of a person whose hair was standing on end because she'd seen the devil. It was too windy to stay out on deck, so we had to move inside. The dance floor was close to where we found a place to stand. Maybe he forgot that he was ashamed to be seen dancing with a tub like me, but when the band struck up "When the Saints Go Marching In," we started dancing automatically. The floor was jammed and the song was fast, so we got kicked a lot. But that wasn't why Bold Robert suddenly stopped dancing. I saw them too. Two guys on the sidelines were watching us dance and laughing. They were drawing wide curves in the air—in the shape of a fat barrel—and pointing at me. At my baby-fat ass.

We pushed through the crowd to the other side of the dance floor.

"Let's go back up on deck," I said. "It's so packed in here."

I was mortified. He was looking over my head, trying to look as if he wasn't with me. "I'll be right back," I said, and headed for the ladies' room.

When I came back, Bold Robert Emmet was dancing with another girl, the one who'd gone swimming with us that afternoon. Her hair was dry and neat in a fetching ponytail. She couldn't have been more than a size 3. She didn't have a curve on her. For all his talk about curves being beautiful, he preferred girls who looked anemic. When the music stopped, they walked to the side and she leaned on the railing around the dance floor, wrote something on a piece of paper, and slowly tucked it into the breast pocket of his shirt. Then Size 3 looked straight at me over Bold Robert's shoulder. She smiled. He'd asked for and she'd given him her phone number, of course. Then he asked her to dance again.

I went back up to the top deck. As the boat moved under the George Washington Bridge, I threw Quinn's school pin into the black river. He could go to hell, I'd go home by myself. I'd lose twenty, no, thirty pounds; he wouldn't recognize me the next time he saw me. And so what if he did? I decided I would not speak to him for one, no, two years, the double-crossing, two-faced bastard.

I got thin fast and fanatically. I enjoyed feeling dizzy and listening to the groaning of my empty stomach in the middle of the night. I cracked the plaster ceilings pounding my butt into the floor five hundred times a day. With my new figure came new friends. Dondi O'Connor had a twenty-inch waist and knew half the Senior class at Xavier Military Academy. "Forget about Regis and what's-his-name," Dondi said. "Only bookworms go there anyway." Maria Mannion, who lived in an eighteen-room apartment on Riverside Drive, who kept cheese glasses of different whiskeys aging on the windowsill of her huge walk-in closet, who had seen *The Seven-Year Itch* seven times, had a brother at Xavier. She said Xavier parties were wild. *"Orgies,* I tell you!" Maria said the word so loud that Fat Josie waddled over to our lunch table, sniffing suspiciously. "Do your mothers know you people don't eat anything for lunch?" she snarled at our bare table.

Dondi O'Connor's party was my first orgy. All I saw when I walked into her dark living room was couples necking. Some necked while they danced, others did it standing up in corners, and two couples were necking on the couch, which was the only piece of furniture in the room. The only light came from a tiny lamp on the floor next to the record player. It glowed like a single lonely vigil light in a dark church. The Platters were singing "Earth Angel." Mannion came over and whispered she'd never seen a Xavier party get hot so fast. Bob Scannell had Dondi in the bedroom and the way the other guys were going, they had One Thing on their minds. She moved away as the biggest hunk in the room put his arms around my waist. "Earth Angel" played again, I put my arms around his neck, and we started to dance. He held me so tight the Poppit pearls spat off my neck onto the bare wood floor. He rubbed his cheek against mine and kept hugging me tighter and massaging my back. No one that big had ever held me so tight before. I hugged him back, as hard as I could, and he put his mouth over my ear and said I was great.

After a few more "dances" we went over to a corner. Mannion was passing around a silver flask of Four Roses. The guy I was with offered Johnny Walker Black Label, but I'd never heard of it so I took a swig of Four Roses because my father used it to make sours and I knew I wouldn't get poisoned. Mannion whispered that the boy I was with was *the* Lieutenant Colonel, the second most important senior at Xavier. (The Colonel was the number one senior.) "But watch out, Girling-hausen. Joe Stallone is also the hottest make-out in New York City. He'll rape you if you give him half a chance."

If I get raped, I thought, my mother will die and it will be her own fault. For Dondi's party she had insisted on making me a red *peau de soir* dress that was too old for me. I'd told her it was cut too low, but she snapped as she always did when I complained about the clothes she made me: "You have no savvy, Martha. Next you'll be picking out gray gabardine." I thought of her and of how dignified the lady on the Vogue pattern envelope looked in my dress as the Lieutenant Colonel mumbled oh my red hot mama and kissed my neck in ten places like a frantically hungry animal. Making out reminded me of the way our cat nuzzled up to you, only the Lieutenant Colonel was no pussycat. He felt strong as a mountain lion.

He showed up at the Academy's Sophomore Tea Dance. Bold Robert Emmet did too, but I ignored him and the other drips from Regis. The Tea Dance was the first time I'd seen the Lieutenant Colonel in his full-dress uniform. Wearing the sword that only the officers were allowed to carry and standing straight beside me as we posed for the yearbook photographs, Joe Stallone looked like one of the nineteenth-century gallants in the portraits hanging upstairs along the Academy's hall-ways. Though he didn't talk much—he was the strong, silent, romantic type—I was positive he was going to invite me to the Xavier Military Ball.

After the Tea Dance, Mannion and her date and the Lieutenant Colonel and I had a few drinks at the Biltmore and then we took a cab out to Angie Battaglia's house in Little Neck, making out all the way.

In Angie's bedroom Mannion and I covered our beard burns with makeup. "God, what a hysterical cab ride. Listen, Girlinghausen, you better watch out. I think Stallone is really horny. God, what a horn!" If somebody or something wasn't "hysterical" to Maria, then he, she, or it was "horny" or a "horn." I thought a horn was like a fink or a square. I horn, you horn, he, she, or it horns.

The only music at the party was soupy Perry Como albums, but it didn't matter because nobody danced. Except for Mannion and her date, everybody was necking. Stallone had me pinned in a corner and was going so hot and heavy he didn't even stop when Angie tapped him on the shoulder and offered us beers. That night was the first time he soul-kissed me and after he did it once he asked me if I minded. I said, "Why should I mind?" At Retreat someone had put a question in the Question Box, "Is soul-kissing a mortal sin, even if you're going steady with the other person?" The priest had gone purple and said, *"Always.* It is *always* mortally sinful, under all circumstances." He told us the story of the couple who'd parked their car on the edge of a cliff. Right after the guy soul-kissed the girl, his knee hit the emergency brake by mistake, and down they plunged, to death and hell for all eternity. The nuns called it "French kissing" and said it was the worst Sin of Impurity you could commit.

I did not believe that God cared about where the Lieutenant Colonel put his tongue. After a while, though, I did think it was a rather monotonous technique, in and out, in and out, like a plunger. And I did not like doing it with someone I did not care about. I was only making believe I liked him just to get him to invite me to the Military Ball.

It was a relief when Angie came up behind us armed with a Polaroid and took our pictures. The flash made Stallone jump as if he'd been ambushed. Then Angie asked everyone to pose together. I held a cigarette in my mouth, a beer in one hand, the Lieutenant Colonel's waist with the other, and raised a leg in the air.

Only Mannion refused to have her picture taken. When we picked up our coats from Angie's bedroom she said, "You're hysterical, Girlinghausen, you're so stupid. Don't you know you never pose for pictures at an orgy?"

The Monday morning after Angie's party the BMT got stuck in the tunnel and I got to school late. Mannion was waiting for me in the garbage room off the Servants' Entrance. We crouched down behind the pails.

"You better turn around and get out of here, Girlinghausen. Play the hook today. Fats got Battaglia in her office first thing this morning and Angie looks like she's gone hysterical. She came into Home Room looking like hell. Little wop rat."

And then along came Josie.

"You trollop," she said to me. "Be in my office at three o'clock."

"You're failing two subjects, Miss Mannion. One more and you're out."

For showing off in front of Angie's Polaroid I suffered the fate of the Woman Taken in Adultery. My mother was dragged in to share my humiliation. Josie must have phoned her at her school and told her to show up for the showdown.

Josie picked up the first stone. "I want to hear your explanation of what went on at Mary Anne O'Connor's party last month. Your daughter's conduct has been reported to me as disgusting, as no better than a tramp's."

"Now just a minute here, Sister." Gertrude wasn't afraid. "Suppose you specify your charges before we go any further."

Josie took aim. "Your daughter not only smokes and drinks. I happen to know that that was a necking party and Martha was the main attraction. I heard she never came up for air the whole night. Of course, the O'Connor girl's parents are divorced. I don't expect her to give a decent party."

"Someone is lying about me," I said. "I've never necked in my life."

"What about the drinking and the smoking?" Josie was cleaning her thumbnail with a paper clip.

"Well, I've had sips of beer. I don't care for cigarettes. My father says smoking is unhealthy."

"What he says is if he ever catches her with one he'll make her eat it! Now then, Sister Marie Joseph. I want to meet Martha's accusers face to face. I expect a public retraction of this slander and *your* apology, Sister."

"All right. Let's forget about the O'Connor girl's party for now." She rocked back and forth in her swivel chair. She aimed again. "Do you deny you disgraced yourself and this school at the affair at Angie Battaglia's house after the Sophomore Tea Dance last Friday?"

"Yes, I do." The old bitch could prove nothing.

"You were not part of any prolonged *kissing* there either? You didn't *touch* any alcoholic beverage?"

"No, Sister, I most certainly did not." It was my word against some stoolpigeon's. There was no proof. "Someone is slandering my name out of spite."

"Perhaps I ought to make it clear, Sister. My husband and I are prepared to bring a lawsuit if necessary to defend our daughter's reputation." My mother narrowed her eyes and thrust her chin forward. I was proud of her for not cringing the way most parents did in front of Josie. She was letting Fats have it right between her tiny pink eyeballs.

But then Josie fired. "Go ahead. Bring a lawsuit. But make sure you show these to your lawyer."

She threw the photographs that Angie had taken with her Polaroid across her desk at us. They landed next to her "Pray Always" sign. "Miss Battaglia was showing them around the coat room this morning as I happened to pass by."

I ducked and said it wasn't me, the girl in the corner necking and the girl with the beer can and her leg in the air, it's somebody else.

I could have cried for my mother. "Well, Sister, this is certainly some situation," she said, holding her hand over her heart as if any minute she might collapse. "When I think of how I raced home from school to make the dress you see in those pictures. There's no fool like an old fool."

"She's on probation for the rest of the year. One more incident like this and she is out the door. She can go to a public school where they let them carry on like tramps."

Fats knew my mother was a public school teacher. She was as dirty a winner as she was a fighter.

That night at home Mother hurled her humiliation at me.

"Liar! Little sneak!" She smacked me for smirking, ordered me to confession, and struck down my social life. "Not another party, do you hear?"

Daddy kept his sense of humor. He looked at the photographs of Martha the Make-out and laughed. "Well, I'll be damned," he said. "Just look at the little devil." I heard him tell Mother that if the nuns tried a little of this they'd be better off. "They're jealous of these kids," he said, and chuckled again.

But Mother was not amused. "I have known it all along: Martha is not the girl Irene is, and she is most certainly not the girl Nony is. Our other two have *principles.*"

The next Saturday she reminded me that confessions at St. Francis started at two o'clock. Father Peabody came at me with a slow curve. I'd recited the usual venial sins, curse words, thirty a day, lies, two hundred a week.

"Anything else?" Through the screen I could see him holding his chin in his hand. I wondered if he ever got so bored he fell asleep.

"Uh, I, uh . . . I commited sins of impurity on several occasions with my boyfriend." God, it was awful. The shame. But like cramps and exams, it would be over fast. As soon as he told me my penance and gave me absolution.

"What do you mean by 'sins of impurity'?"

I could feel my face burning scarlet.

"Uh, well, necking, Father. At parties."

"How old are you?"

"Fifteen."

"How long did you say it's been since your last confession?"

"A month."

"Was it passionate necking?"

"Uh, I guess so."

"You *guess?* Confession is not the place to guess. Was there soul-kissing?"

He was worse than the dentist. Suddenly I had to go to the bathroom in the worst way.

"Yes, Father."

"How many times?"

"Three. Three times." Thirty-three was closer to the truth, but if I told him that the shock of saying it out loud would explode my bowels all over the confessional.

"Did you enjoy it?"

"No, Father." I couldn't remember whether I did or I didn't.

"Well, you should thank God, and resolve never to commit this particular sin again."

"Yes, Father." More than anything I wanted to ask him if the bathroom in the church basement was open on Saturday afternoons.

But though Father Peabody held the record for saying the fastest Low Mass in the parish, he heard confessions thoroughly.

"Did you sin with any other part of your body?" he asked.

"No."

"Do you know what petting is?"

"No, Father." *Of course I do, stupid. It means petting, or patting, the way you pat a baby or a doll.*

"Did he touch you on the breast?"

He wasn't holding his chin anymore. He was as alert as a cat trailing a robin. His question made my ears sting and my head pound. I saw in my mind the Lieutenant Colonel touching my breast. I felt as ashamed as I would have if it had actually happened, if someone whom I didn't give a damn about and who didn't give a damn about me had touched me there.

"Did he touch you below your waist? Did you fondle one another?"

I couldn't help it. I farted. Good and loud, and oh God, it smelled.

He gave me absolution so fast you'd think I was dying. I made it to the church john just in time. I swore to God I'd never go near that prying son of a bitch again.

My mother would have been right at home in the early church when sinners had to earn forgiveness by performing extreme public penances. Henry IV had to walk barefoot across a snow-covered Europe before the Pope lifted the ban of excommunication; I had to iron twelve tablecloths and ninety-six napkins on seven dateless weekends before she believed my purpose of amendment was firm. As Canossa won the Pope back to the frostbitten Henry's side, Valentine's Day softened my mother. She turned me loose from the ironing board to go to Judy McQuillan's party. "But mark my words: you're only getting out because I know the McQuillan girl's parents. And you be home in this house by eleven o'clock or you will not put a foot out that door for the rest of your life."

But at eleven o'clock the Lieutenant Colonel and I were wrapped up so tight in a corner of McQuillan's cellar that I knew I was in for another lonely penitential season. He claimed me before I was halfway down the cellar stairs. As I stopped in the stairwell to check my straps, I saw him coming toward me, holding out his arms. Like a miracle, "Earth Angel" came on the record player.

There was no liquor at the party, but every couple was making out as if it were the Passion Play of the season. From what I could see, Dondi O'Connor opened her mouth at least every five seconds. The Lieutenant Colonel was hotter that night than he'd ever been. When he bit me on the shoulder I almost said Hey, lay off, but biting was a new trick, a funny one really, and I wanted to find out for myself all the tricks that went with making out. Also I was a little scared of Joe Stallone. It was too late to pull a Maria Goretti. When, a little later, he said, "Scannell is taking Dondi back to her apartment in Jackson Heights—let's go with them," I was afraid to back out. Bob Scannell had already asked Dondi to the Military Ball. I said good-bye to Judy McQuillan and to her parents and got my coat.

As I took it off in Dondi's dark, bare apartment, I saw a mirage of my mother's face and in my head heard her screaming at me. *Mark My Words . . .* So I faced the music and called home, hoping Daddy would answer. But she picked it up, and I could tell she didn't have her teeth in which gave me nerve. I told her the party had ended at eleven but that Mr. McQuillan had only driven us as far as Dondi O'Connor's apartment in Jackson Heights and I hadn't had a chance to call before now and anyway all the girls were staying over at Dondi's and please could I stay too?

She may have had only her gums working, but she came through as strong as a meat cleaver.

"Are you going to catch it when I get my hands on you." She slammed down the phone.

When I went back into the living room, Dondi and Scannell had disappeared. There was only the Lieutenant Colonel sitting on the edge of what had been a sofa but was now opened out into a double bed. He had taken off his shoes and tie. First we necked standing up, then sitting down, and before I knew it I was flat on my back. Then he sprawled himself on top of me. I didn't care for the arrangement because it made me feel at his mercy. And the way he was going, he was no one to trust. He was panting and snorting and bucking like the horse that threw me in Central Park. The harder he kissed me, the more leery I felt. He was hurting me. He tried to unzip my dress, but I wriggled out of his hands. And then he started in on Father Peabody's specialty, fondling below the waist.

I was too afraid to stop him. To him I was nothing. He wouldn't care whether I liked what he was doing or not. He'd never asked me out on a real date, we'd never had a conversation. I only knew he drank Black Label and was very proud of his Xavier sword. We were like two stray mutts rolling on the grass in Bowne Park. To get invited to the Military Ball, I had led him on. Now I was getting what I deserved. Stallone lifted up my dress then and fumbled at my garter belt. I said "Wait" and jumped up off the bed as if I was going to do something fancy. He got up on the other side and turned his back to me. I'd have been happy to sink his sword between his shoulder blades if that would have gotten me out of there. *He'll rape you if you give him half a chance* . . . Maria Mannion had warned me. I could tell from the way he was breathing he had made up his mind. This was to be the night and the place and the bitch. I'm going to get raped, I thought. There was no way out. If I fought him, he was big enough to break my neck. Instead of going to a fancy dance, I was about to do time in a home for unwed mothers. Stallone had taken off his belt and shirt. I was alone with a rapist.

Then, as the cream of Xavier Military Academy unzipped his fly and began to step out of his trousers, the doorbell of Dondi's apartment rang. "I'll get it," I said fast. He lunged for his shirt and tripped over his pants which were half on and half off. I ran before he could catch me and force me to shut up till whoever was out there went away. I opened the door, feeling delivered. There, with her gray hair flying, her nightgown hanging below her coat was my mother. She looked like a hag out of hell.

"Get your coat."

Out on the sidewalk, she smacked me, she screamed at me, all the way home through Corona and five red lights. She threatened me with a boarding school in the Berkshires. She hadn't believed my story on the phone, so she'd checked with the McQuillans and caught me red-handed. "I'd have driven all night if necessary. Do not think your father and I are going to sit home like a pair of fools and let you ruin yourself and your future. If you can't amount to anything now, I'll make sure you amount to something later on . . ."

Back home she howled like a banshee for over an hour. She

was Shelley Winters, Ma Kettle, and Lady Macbeth in one fantastic package. "As far as parties go, you little sneak, you are finished, all washed up. Is that clear? Don't ask because the answer will be no." Then she took out her teeth for the second time that night and went to bed.

Well, of course I could never tell her, and never would I thank her, but this screeching witch of a mother was my angel of deliverance. While the Pharaoh had had his back turned and his pants down, she'd opened the Red Sea and brought me home safe. *Home Free All.*

Nony took after my mother. She was very sure of what was right and what was wrong. She always seemed to know how to act.

That Easter vacation my mother dragged us down to Colonial Williamsburg in Virginia. A real schoolteacher, she almost killed us Good Friday afternoon she was so busy pointing out the Susquehanna River—she missed a curve in Route 40 and that was the end of our car. We continued by Greyhound.

In the bus terminal at Richmond we had to wait a few hours for the Williamsburg bus, enough time for a long first snootful of Jim Crow—black and white Cokes, black and white water fountains, black and white johns, as if shit comes in different colors. The waiting room was filled with Negro families and white men studying their racing forms. It was as quiet as a city church on a rainy Sunday night.

So you would have thought that people would have jumped

up at the awful sound that all of a sudden gashed the silence. A Negro man fell and hit his head on the concrete floor. He groaned and rolled around wildly, first clutching at himself with his arms and then flailing them around desperately. But not a soul moved. At first everyone stared at him. A few said, "Tsk, tsk, tsk," and shook their heads. I stared at his torn clothes and the white stubble on his brown face and thought he must be a drunk, like the men on the Bowery.

Then I heard Nony shout. "That man is an epileptic." She dug into her pocketbook, jumped up, and ran to him. As I said, Nony knew how to act.

"Get a policeman," she yelled. By the time a cop came, a Negro minister had taken control of the epileptic. He was sitting on top of him and Nony was holding his tongue down with the toothbrush she used to brush her eyebrows with.

Nony told the cop to get an ambulance fast. Maybe she was able to see the right thing to do and do it without being afraid of making an ass of herself, because she didn't waste her energy breaking rules and covering her tracks. That night in Richmond she knew the right thing to do as surely as you know if the weather is hot or cold. I hadn't budged when the Negro fell. Nony, I was sure, would never let anyone soul-kiss her or rape her just to get invited to a dance. I wondered how it was that she had turned out good and I was no better than all the other sleazy people in the waiting room. "You're not worth your salt," Nony once said to me in a fight.

. . . And the latest is—she smokes! I found grains of tobacco in her coat pocket. Irene, I must get her away from the good-for-nothings she calls her friends over the summer. May I send her down to you? I can tell you it's been one frightful year our youngest has put us through. I worry about what will become of her. Is it possible that Martha is the one we used to call our Littlest Angel? Put her to work, will you? It's what she needs to knock some sense into her. . . .

I read mother's letter to my oldest sister and exulted. Irene and Steve lived in Pennsylvania on a lovely hillside in the Alleghanies. Irene was expecting her fourth baby in midsummer. The first three babies—Edward, age three, Mark, age two, and Sarah, age one—I adored (though Irene told me, when I was little, that only God was adorable). I described their every new trick and syllable to my lunch table at school, showing snapshots and quoting Irene's weekly letters. I cared more about Sarah's teething and what Mark said to the mailman than about any detail of life at Xavier, Regis, or Loyola Prep. I covered this up, however, for I thought that having one's niece and nephews always in one's heart, instead of a boy, made me a freak. My mother meant a summer at Irene and Steve's as a punishment for my sophomore sins; but I could think of no greater reward on earth than a six-week stretch of diapering, feeding, and rocking the three darling babies I pretended were mine.

I turned my St. Francis Assisi school ring around to look like a wedding band the afternoons I walked the children up and down the roads of Churchill Valley. That was the name of the development Irene and Steve lived in. Most of the women we passed on our walks didn't look much older than me. They had names like Neatsy and Annie Mae and May-ry, and they treated me like a celebrity because I came from New York. When clouds and thunder rolled over the valley, they said, with a wonderful twang, "Hey, May-ry! It's clabberin' up to *down.*"

It never downed once while Irene waited for her one, two, three-week overdue baby. There was no breeze either, and Steve got so fidgety he couldn't concentrate on preparing his classes. He taught Philosophy at Aquinas College in Wilkes-Barre. He sat around slurping coffee and entertaining Irene by reading out loud all the dumb answers he'd gotten from his students on their final exam in Metaphysics. All the dumbbells were girls, which made Steve roar after each dramatic reading, "Once again Saint Thomas is proven right: a woman's place is in the sink." Irene smiled at him sort of numbly during these sessions, as she hauled her big stomach from the stove to the kitchen table to the refrigerator to the sink and then upstairs to the rocker where in a tired voice she sang Sarah to sleep. *"Speed bonnie boat like a bird on the wing . . . over the sea to Skye . . ."*

One night, while I was reading myself to sleep downstairs on the living room sofa, I heard all hell break loose upstairs. At first I thought Irene must be having the baby. Then as I lay listening to thumps, stamping, slamming drawers, Oh no you don't from Irene, Steve's racking pipe cough, I realized they were having a fight. It sounded like it was over a dresser drawer. First one of them pulled it open, and then the other one landed out of bed, stomped across the floor, and banged it shut. It happened again and again, the banging getting more furious each time. Then, suddenly, the house became quiet. I lay stiff all night, dreading that the fight might start again. Toward dawn they came downstairs and tiptoed through the living room and left for the hospital. They named the baby

Gerard because his head was so big Irene screamed for the first time since her first delivery and promised St. Gerard, the Patron Saint of Mothers, *anything* if he'd only help her.

The rains finally came the day Irene brought baby Gerard home from the hospital. And that night Steve's colleagues came from the college's Theology Study Group. They brought along their pipes and wives, who, with one exception, were pregnant and wore Bermuda shorts, which made their varicose veins show. They frowned a lot while they listened to their husbands' talk, as if what they were talking about was very very difficult to understand. Listening to the rusty dusty way the men talked about Adam and Eve, the topic of that night's discussion, I yawned and wondered how their students ever stayed awake for seventy-five-minute lectures. It baffled me that these pipe-sucking bores were the same people whom Irene bragged about in her letters as their brilliant, stimulating friends from the university.

I escaped by taking some tea upstairs to Irene. I found her sprawled across their four-poster bed, crying. She'd stayed in the hospital only two days and I guess she was still recovering from having the baby. One of the children woke up then and after I rocked him, he stopped crying. But every screen in the house had holes the size of silver dollars, so the mosquitoes kept pouring in and waking up one after another of the children. I sat in the dark, humid heat, rocking Edward and Mark and Sarah by turns. I fell asleep in the rocker and woke up in the middle of the night but not from the whine of mosquitoes.

I heard Irene moan and sort of scream, but their bedroom door was closed so I knew Steve had come up to bed and I figured he'd help her. All of a sudden he came busting out of the bedroom and stamped downstairs. But he didn't come back with medicine for her or a bottle for the baby. I could smell that he'd lit his pipe. I heard him stalking around the living room. Irene was sobbing so hard the bed springs were creaking.

At home, Irene had been in constant trouble with Mother and Daddy, mostly for keeping her bedroom like a pigsty, and here she was in trouble again. Over what, I had no idea. But from the sound of her, I thought her heart was breaking. I tried to think of how I could help her, but I knew an outsider could do nothing. I went into the bathroom and cried for her till the sun came up red-hot. The first thing it touched was the tributary of the Allegheny River that cut through the bottom of Churchill Valley. *River sister, don't cry. Red river sister, dear, dear sister . . .*

Over that summer Marymound Academy underwent a metamorphosis. As if a slug began to strut like a peacock, the school day suddenly took on personality. Her name was Sister Miriam. She had two grand entrances every day.

She came on first at 11:00 A.M. to teach us Junior Year Religion. She swished the skirts of her habit into our classroom as if it were a concert hall. We were her audience and she was the virtuoso the whole world was talking about. The required Religion textbook, *Faith Through the Ages,* was so dull, she said, so pedestrian. She stashed it behind a drapery and improvised. She taught the sacraments by pirouetting around something she called "a sacramental world view" and singing out lines from the poetry of William Butler Yeats— "We are blessed by everything,/Everything we look upon is blessed." One day she rushed in and threw open the French windows. Stepping out on the balcony and inhaling the air of Sixty-eighth Street, she exclaimed, " 'There lives the dearest freshness deep down things'—those are the words of Gerard Manley Hopkins and the best definition of grace I know." Some days she read aloud from *The Seven Storey Mountain,* the autobiography of Thomas Merton. She used it as a warm-up exercise for her own ecstatic monologues on the spiritual life. Her face, the most beautiful nun's face we had ever seen—in person or in the "Come Follow Me" brochures put out by the religious orders—grew flushed as she leaped from faith to hope to charity. She was all passionate sincerity; we were sure that anyone whose eyes could shine over religion the way hers did, who could make it sound so beautiful and romantic must have had a tragic love affair. Her lover must have died young or maybe she and Thomas Merton had been lovers before they both renounced the world and entered the religious life.

We felt embarrassed and strangely thrilled to hear her speak about her life as the "Bride of Christ." We'd heard other nuns brag about their mystical marriages, but because they were so fang-toothed and molely, they made the idea sound weird. But Sister Miriam blushed like a real bride as she whispered forth the bliss of each of her three vows. It was poverty that gave her the Franciscan habit she loved so much, holy poverty that let her wear her bridal gown every day instead of only once like an ordinary bride. The times she spoke about the habit, she kissed her scapular or rubbed it against her cheek.

The vow of chastity . . . chastity was freedom, she said. "It's a very passionate, turbulent vow. Chastity is not the cold lonely hell of fiction. Though I guess it can be if you're not right for it." She told us that if we wanted to understand the beauty of virginity we should go up to the Cloisters and look at the Unicorn tapestries. "Especially the 'Unicorn in Captivity.' It's the best evocation of . . . well, marriage, really, that I know of. The marriage of Christ and the Virgin and the marvelous freedom the vow of chastity gives . . ."

The only thing Sister Miriam had to say about the vow of obedience was that it could be a crucible. She made each vow, each part of the habit, and the very word *vocation* sound mysterious and sort of romantic. After eleven years of dumpy nuns who waddled and bullied, one hour of this six-foot tall goddess was enough to spellbind, to make you almost forget that other nuns were not like her.

Our section of the Junior class got to be spellbound through two performances a day. Sister Miriam came again at two o'clock for last period English, usually a time for sneaking a nap, no matter what the subject. But if she gushed over Religion, in English class she gave out like a waterfall. The heavy oak door opened with a bang and she swung in—like Loretta Young, tossing her head and calling:

> *The soul selects her own society,*
> *Then shuts the door;*
> *On her divine majority*
> *Obtrude no more.*

Then she slammed the classroom door and for sixty minutes brought to life Emily Dickinson, "the nun of Amherst," or whatever other writer she felt like talking about that day.

She awed me. She was the first nun I'd ever had who knew anything more than what was in a teacher's manual. And she loved what she knew, the way Bold Robert Emmet loved singing and my father loved his operas.

After school we sat in the Dirty Deli and speculated about where she'd come from and why someone who looked like her would become a nun. Nina Iondola from Queens Village, who had read the *Rule of St. Benedict* and the *Life of St. Teresa of Avila* and who wanted to be a Carmelite herself, said that Sister Miriam's vocation was no more mysterious than anyone else's.

"God called her; that's all there is to it. She had no choice. That's the way a religious vocation works." Nina played with the three gold rings on her ring finger. They were friendship rings with Christ, she said.

The year before Sister Miriam came to the Academy, Mannion and Dondi and I had gone to the Deli to smoke and gossip about the Xavier boys. Now, as each day through the month of September the gossip ran not to boys but to the new celebrity in a habit, Mannion got more and more disgusted.

"Oh shove it, Nina," she yelled at the end of one of Nina's lectures. The men from the FBI around the corner on Sixty-ninth Street stared at us from their table in the corner. "This is *my* Deli. I discovered it while you were off going hysterical to Jesus somewhere. Stop turning it into a goddamn convent. You are forbidden to talk about nuns in my Deli from this day forward."

But by the end of October, Nina and the rest of us were still fascinated by Sister Miriam. So after school Mannion started going to a luncheonette on Eighty-fifth Street where the Regis boys hung out.

Mr. and Mrs. Rubin, the Jewish couple who ran the Deli, asked each day, "Where's Maria? What happened to our best customer? She used to come in here even on weekends. What's the matter, did you girls have an argument or something?" Marlene Rubin wanted to know what our new "religion kick" was all about.

"Everyday it's nuns and Sister So-and-So. Last year it was boys. Till dark, Martha, you used to sit here, you and Maria and Dondi, talking nothing but boys. We used to worry about you going home so late. That Martha, I used to say to myself, she'll be married before she graduates. Boys—that was normal. But nuns . . . Who? What?"

Nina tried to explain the purpose of religious life to Marlene, but the whole time Nina talked, Marlene shook her head.

"It sounds *unnatural,*" Marlene said. That was the word my father always used about the nuns. *"They ought to use their bodies for what they were made for instead of covering them up . . . maybe if they had some kids of their own they wouldn't torture everyone else's."*

Mr. Rubin agreed with his wife and my father. "Nina, Nina, let me tell you something. Get yourself a nice husband and have children. That goes for the rest of you too. What more can you want?"

After they went back behind the counter, Nina said the Rubins didn't understand monasticism, especially the vow of chastity, because they were Jewish. Jews, she said, thought sex was all of life, instead of just one part. They thought virginity was something funny.

Nina wagged her index finger at us as if she was a great theologian, and divinely inspired.

Sister Miriam did not always entertain us with poetry. One day she wept, at first softly, and then in fury as she hurled a book across the room. She had been reading aloud from *The Seven Storey Mountain* and she'd started to cry when she got to the part about the death of Merton's younger brother. But some of us in the back of the room had started to laugh a few pages before she got to that part and she hadn't noticed. We'd cracked up because Thomas Merton had mentioned Douglaston, which was where Dondi O'Connor's boyfriend came from. Sister Miriam thought we were laughing about Merton's brother dying.

Her tantrum could not have been less nunny. For overall histrionics, it matched any fit my mother had ever thrown, except that Sister Miriam looked more gorgeous the more she screamed and sobbed.

"You little *bitches,*" she blurted. "You insensitive little bitches."

Sister Jane Agnes's eighth grade fit had been cold and scary. Fat Josie's fits were as predictable as a bad-tempered sow's. But Sister Miriam made me feel sorry for her and sorry that we'd been so silly about Douglaston: the way she was carrying on she *must* have known Thomas Merton. If they ever made a movie about him and her, she could play herself. She was holding one hand over her mouth. Her black eyebrows arched dramatically and her tears spotted the bib of her habit.

Then she sat down at the desk and buried her face in her hands the way some fanatics do after Communion. When she came back up a few minutes later, she apologized. While she dried her long black lashes, she explained that her nerves were shot because she was up every night till the wee hours studying for her doctoral exams at Catholic University. Just that morning during Meditation she'd broken down in chapel for no reason. Sister Cecilia had been so sweet, she'd put her back to bed and brought her tea after Mass.

"You'll have to be patient with me," Sister Miriam said. "I have no time to prepare for classes and I'll never see my way clear to marking your compositions till after the orals in November. How in God's name am I supposed to find time to act as moderator of the school newspaper I haven't the foggiest. You cannot imagine what the pressure is like. Not only the academic pressure of having to be familiar with all of English literature from *Beowulf* to T. S. Eliot, but the pressure, the responsibility I feel as a religious—I am the first sister in our community to be sent for a doctorate. If I fail . . ."

Well, we sat there feeling like turds for having made her cry. The class president, sounding a bit weepy herself, apologized for the whole class. She also made a suggestion: perhaps it would help Sister to use our English class as a time to rehearse for her orals—she could practice on us, sort of tell us about works of literature and their authors.

Sister Miriam's eyes filled up again. She said that she had heard for years from every sister who had ever been stationed at the Academy how kind and sweet Academy girls were. Now she knew it for herself.

"It's because the Blessed Sacrament is in the building," she said. "It's because you live in the presence of God that you're all so good."

That was a new twist. Until then, I'd thought the only thing most Academy girls were good at was keeping the rules and ratting on those who broke them.

Now that we knew she had no time for us we stopped wondering when she'd return the compositions she collected from us every week. I'd been slaving over mine, though I knew the writing of a high school girl could only bore her. Her life, she told us, was literature. She loved literature more than anything else in the world, except, of course, being a Franciscan Sister. Her two loves had something in common. Religious life was supposed to lead to sanctity and that's exactly what literature had to give: the sanctity of truth —a special kind of truth that nothing else gives in the same way. And the poet, like the priest and the prophet, reveals his truth to men who have the grace of understanding. Daily she invoked the names of her favorite poet-saints the way other nuns rattled off the names of the Seven Capital Sins. Eliot and Yeats and Pound she adored. D. H. Lawrence she thought sentimental but one of the greats all the same.

> *Not every man has flowers in his house*
> *In soft September, at slow, sad Michaelmas.*

By quoting him with reverence, she made Lawrence and all the writers she loved sound like saints whose books were holy.

Maria Mannion and a few other girls were not impressed. At the lunch table they tore her apart.

"Do you suppose Sister Miriam will ever come off her high

horse and prepare us for the English Regents the way she's supposed to?"

"What gets me," Elizabeth Filippi whined, "is the way she shows off. And all that disgusting *poetry.* Who cares about poetry?"

"Sister Miriam is sick," Mannion said. "My sister went so hysterical when I told her my English teacher recommended D. H. Lawrence. Kathy said her English professor at St. John's says he's pure filth. At St. John's they call him 'Life Below the Belt Lawrence.' If I flunk the English Regents, honest to Christ, I'll write a letter to the goddamn Mother General. I'll be goddamned if I'll go to summer school because of an English teacher who did nothing all year but throw tantrums and rave about dirty books."

The week after the Hungarian revolution, Sister Miriam pitched a fit that was as good as a play. It made very clear that Sisters in Christ were not always sisters at heart.

Sister Theophane, the nun who taught us French the period before Sister Miriam arrived for English, was the Academy's most militant anti-Communist and a self-appointed apologist for the censured Senator McCarthy. She was always circulating petitions to have him uncensored and trying to get us to demonstrate at the Fortieth Street pier against ships that carried goods from Communist countries.

A few days after the Hungarian revolution, Theophane came to class followed by a parade of sophomores from her Home Room. They carried cartons full of mimeographed petitions demanding that Eisenhower send U.S. troops to help the Hungarian Freedom Fighters. Not only did she require everyone to take one hundred of them and get them filled with signatures, she canceled all homework assignments if we'd promise to join the crowd that was demonstrating down the block outside the Russian Consulate.

"Soon, *mes élèves,* I assure you: Moscow will be marching down Fifth Avenue and the first thing they'll do is hang your own Franciscan Sisters from the lampposts." Goody, goody, I thought. How about Fat Josie from the flagpole over the Central Park Zoo?

Theophane was in such a flurry about Hungary and the petitions and World Communism that when the bell signaled the end of class she flew out the door as if she were wanted at the barricades and forgot to take her petitions with her. Sister Miriam arrived for English class and found them scattered all over the top of the teacher's desk. After the opening prayer she brushed the whole pile of them onto the floor. She muttered something about getting this trash out of her sight. After one of Theophane's pets picked the petitions up off the floor, Sister Miriam took them out of her arms, opened the French window, and stepped out onto the balcony overlooking Sixty-eighth Street. She threw Sister Theophane's petitions into the air and recited:

> *The blood-dimmed tide is loosed, and everywhere*
> *The ceremony of innocence is drowned;*
> *The best lack all conviction, while the worst*
> *Are full of passionate intensity.*

Most of our pro-Hungary but anti-Theophane class applauded. As we ran to the other windows we saw that the wind was carrying the petitions down Sixty-eighth Street and onto the sidewalks around the Russian Consulate on the corner.

Then Sister Miriam told Mannion and the rest of them who were giving her hate looks to put the remaining cartons of litter out in the hall and to stay out there until they wiped the sour looks off their pusses.

After school, in the Deli, Nina Iondola and I hashed over Sister Miriam's performance.

"Of course, what she does on her own, throwing Sister Theophane's propaganda away like that, doesn't mean anything." Nina lowered her voice as if it were important that our conversation not be overheard by the FBI men at the next table. "Do you know that Sister Miriam's Superior could order her to sign that petition and she'd have to do it? She could even order her to vote for Eisenhower and she'd have to obey even if she was for Stevenson."

"I don't believe it."

"She most certainly would. That's the whole principle behind the vow of obedience. You surrender your own conscience to do the will of God as it is manifested in your Superior." She wagged her index finger at me as she lectured. Nina wore no makeup over the black circles she got from meditating all night and running to Mass at dawn.

"But that's like Nazis," I said. "Heil Hitler, even though you know in your gut he's nuts—*that's* the will of God?"

"The whole question of free will is a very difficult one for philosophers as well as for theologians. It's a great paradox, really. A nun is free to choose not to be free."

"Paradox" was one of Sister Miriam's favorite words. I watched Nina's profile in the mirror as she talked. When I looked at her I thought of the Mona Lisa and also of the word *chastity.* Her father wanted her to marry Giovanni Fanfanni, a rich importer. Nina vowed to run away forever if Mr. Iondola got Giovanni to propose.

"It does sound insane," I said. "But when you think of the whole thing as a paradox, well, it's more interesting. Then it almost sounds like poetry in a way."

"Exactly! You see, Martha, the monastic search for perfection," she said, inhaling deeply through a black cigarette holder, "has been humanity's greatest adventure." The smoke came out of her and drifted upward like incense.

Like Sister Miriam, Nina made her private mystical life seem exotic. After school as we were walking to the library or someplace, all of a sudden she'd duck into St. Patrick's, or whatever church we happened to be passing, as if her lover was waiting for her in every tabernacle in the city. While she prayed she closed her eyes and lifted her sallow face toward the altar, sometimes looking as if she was about to die of cramps, most of the time as if she was waiting to be kissed.

"Come with me," she said one afternoon. "I want to show you the most beautiful place in New York City."

We took the A train up to the Medical Center at 168 Street and Broadway and then walked east to High Bridge Park. We climbed toward the water tower at the top of a hill. Halfway up, Nina stopped and turned around. "There it is," she said, pointing. I looked down and saw the Harlem River spanned by a few spunky-looking bridges. To the south I saw the Triborough. On the opposite bank of the river the Bronx rose like a separate city on a hazy bluff.

"Pretty good," I said. "How did you find this spot?"

"That sandstone building over there, the one by itself, with the cross on the roof. That's the place."

"What about it?"

"I told you. That is the most beautiful place in New York. It's the Carmelite monastery I'm going to enter. If I'm received. The professed sisters vote on you. I may have to go to college for two years first. You see contemplative orders are much more selective about their candidates than active ones." She took my arm. "You mustn't tell a soul at school about this," she whispered.

How could I make fun of her for liking a monastery when my own favorite place in the city was the Cloisters, a monastery made into a museum, on the next river over.

"Let's climb to the water tower. The view must be even better from up there."

"No, Martha. I think I'll stay down here. I'd like to be alone for a few minutes. You go."

I did, and when I came back she was sitting on the ground with her eyes closed. I knew she was praying again, probably that she would be accepted by the monastery. But she looked like a heroine in an opera, Carmen or Lucia or somebody, about to burst into an aria while she waited for Don Juan in their secret wooded meeting place.

> *Two paradises 'twere in one*
> *To live in paradise alone.*

Sister Miriam quoted those lines of Andrew Marvell when she was fed up about something. I thought of them the times after school when I went places by myself, usually to the library. The treetops on both sides of Fifth arched a leafy vault over the avenue, making it the world's longest, most pigeony nave, its high altar the arch of Washington Square. The street had an echo. Out of a sudden swirl of dead leaves or kids quarreling over swings in Central Park came a voice as even as a chorus.

There lives the dearest freshness deep down things.

Like poets and prophets, the rooftops proclaimed life a gift, used by wise men to build the city. "Wise Man Fish Here" said the sign outside the Gotham Book Mart: inside an old woman with thick white coronet braids went about her work with the same concentration I'd seen in the doctor who saved my father's life and in the conductors of symphonies. At the Forty-second Street library, before I settled down to read something, I often looked through books on careers, but they were as dull as the etiquette books we used in Charm Class.

Nony had still not decided on a career, though she was a sophomore in college. I was sure she was going to be a nun. When she was in high school, I'd found a brochure in her pocketbook that said "Be ye perfect as your heavenly Father is perfect" on the cover, under the picture of a beautiful nun carrying a crucifix. I thought Nony was perfect enough to be the nun on the cover without having to actually join a convent. She dated boys who respected her—they took her to Jahn's Ice Cream Parlor after school dances, not to beer halls and dark apartments—and she had never in her life said a four-letter word. She sang "like an angel out of heaven" in Daddy's words and was a brilliant pianist. Her music teachers thought she was Juilliard material and were furious when she accepted a scholarship to Cherry Hill College, a concentration camp in Westchester that did not even have a music department. Cherry Hill billed itself as the finest liberal arts college for Catholic women in New York State. Nony loved the place. She was always inviting me up for the weekend. I went once.

Friday night we went to a "Talk Without Chalk." The guest speaker was a McCarthyite. The only time the girls in the audience looked up from their knitting was when a Cherry Hill philosophy teacher interrupted the speaker and started shouting and waving his pipe, calling the speaker "a dangerous voice, a right-winger to his underwear." The other teachers sitting with him sucked their pipes furiously, reminding me of my brother-in-law and his cronies at Aquinas. Nony said there was no resemblance at all: Steve was a creep, whereas the Cherry Hill faculty were fine, liberal people—"Gentlemen," she said, "in Cardinal Newman's sense of the word."

We went to a Mixer. Afterwards, when I told Nony about the blimp from Iona, an aspiring parole officer, whom I'd gotten stuck with all night, she prickled with Cherry Hill charity. "You know, Martha, you're very hard on people. Who are you to be so choosy?" She could afford to be kind. She was going with a fabulous-looking creature from Fairfield that year and didn't have to swallow the humiliations of the Saturday Night Mixer. I lay awake in her roommate's bed, wishing someone like Bold Robert Emmet or even the Lieutenant Colonel were lying beside me. In the middle of the night I knelt in the corduroyed window seat and watched the nightwatchwoman making her rounds. Armed with a map of the campus, she gave out demerits to the rooms that had lights on after eleven o'clock. I swore to Christ I would never, under any circumstances, incarcerate myself at the College of Cherry Hill.

When I phoned to thank Nony for the great college weekend, she told me the nuns had fired the philosophy teacher who had attacked the McCarthyite at the "Talk Without Chalk." The faculty was up in arms over it, but there was nothing they could do. They had their own jobs to protect. "The nuns are holding all the trumps," she said.

She chose the perfect image. Maybe it was an inside campus joke, but a lot of Cherry Hill girls, when you asked them what their major was, said "Bridge!" And a lot of Cherry Hillers did seem to be in training for a lifetime career: they played bridge mornings before breakfast, through entire afternoons, and after lights out, under the twenty-five watt bulb in the john, masked in Ponds and wearing their aqua bathrobes and white wooly crew socks.

Sister Miriam passed her orals with honors. The rest of the year she was preoccupied with studying for her comprehensives, but she did find time to start marking our compositions. One afternoon, in a melodramatic voice, she read aloud an example of "purple prose" from Elizabeth Filippi's paper. Sister Miriam's eyes said what they always said when she read out samples of our writing—What dreadful stuff. I made a face as if to say Yeah, what garbage, save us from purple prose.

She saw my look and slowly she began to turn purple. "I'd like to see you after school this afternoon, Martha. I've had enough of your distracting looks." She threw the paper on the desk of the purple prosist. "I am angry!" she yelled in her beautiful passionate voice. Then she stalked out of the class-room.

At three o'clock I told her I couldn't stay because I had to be at work by three-thirty. Though my parents were taking it for granted I'd follow Nony to Cherry Hill, I was working as a wrapper at Saks to earn enough to pay the tuition at a college I picked out myself. Sister Miriam had calmed down since her explosion in the classroom. "That's okay, Martha," she said. "Come see me at eight tomorrow morning. I've got a few things to talk to you about that I've wanted to say all year." She sounded as if she really cared about me. Her tone of voice reminded me of Irene's when she acted like she was glad I was her little sister.

At work I was so nervous at the thought of having to face her alone that I forgot to put the belts in with the dresses and bathrobes I wrapped. Just before closing time my supervisor discovered the belts under my counter. She sent me to the basement to retrieve all the beltless boxes I'd sent down the chute. I stood underneath the mountain of cartons ready for United Parcel, wondering what it would be like to face Sister Miriam alone. Because I knew I could never think of intelli-gent enough things to say to her, I had kept my distance all year long—I'd never dared speak to her outside of class. Once I'd planned to ask her to explain *The Sound and the Fury* to me. I'd spent Sunday night memorizing the words I'd use to ask her. But I lost my nerve by Monday afternoon and instead of going up to her after class, I played hookey the next day and reread the book on a bench in front of the seal fountain in Central Park.

For a second the next morning, I thought she had forgotten that she'd told me to come in early. When I walked into the classroom, she was lost in some kind of dream world, sitting at her desk under the painting of the Sacred Heart. She looked up at me, still holding open the book she'd been reading.

"We were the last romantics," she said. That was like Irene too. You could tell Irene her spaghetti sauce was great, but out of the blue she'd quote some airy fairy line at you.

Then Sister Miriam snapped her book closed and without a pause she asked me why on earth I was so unfriendly toward her.

"You never stay after school the way the other girls do." My having an after-school job made no difference to her. She said I acted stand-offish toward her all the time. She reminded me of the time she waved to me at a lecture at N.Y.U. and I made believe I hadn't seen her. Then she brought up how snotty I could be toward some of the girls in my class. "If looks could kill, Martha, those poor things would have died long ago because of you. You know, you'll never be a happy woman if you stick only to your own little group. Unless you make yourself be kind to the people who interest you least you'll dry up like an old maid."

I could hear the early birds who showed up before the first bell every day to water Sister's plants scratching outside the closed classroom door. What if one of them walked in and saw the embarrassment blotched all over my face?

I defended myself. "I don't do anything to hurt them. I just stay clear of them. They bore me." She was the one who was always saying how Longfellow *bored* her, politicians *bored* her, our compositions *bored* her.

"But *charity*, my dear child—" She moved toward me and stood over my desk. She looked down at me earnestly, as if she cared terribly that I listen to her, the way Nony looked when she sang in a concert. Then one of the a-k-ing early birds opened the classroom door and peeked in. "Oops! "Scuse *me*, Sister." I knew she'd seen my face, chastened, and as red as Sister Miriam's.

She didn't stop talking. "If I had withheld myself from the other Sisters in the community, Martha, from the ones who seem the most insignificant, I never would have lasted in the convent, never. Unless you have charity in your heart, you'll wither away before you're thirty."

I'd never seen a nun up that close since the first grade. She didn't have the Baby Powdery nun's smell, but her hands were the usual soft waxy clean, and her forehead had the mean-looking crease from the stiff headpiece of the habit that held her brains in. When she asked me to try to be friendlier to all the girls, not only to her, I might as well have been wearing a collar as tight as hers. I practically choked I was so embarrassed. "I'll try," I said. But I wanted to say what I always said to Nony when she told me to be nice to people we couldn't stand. "It's hypocritical, being nice to people you really don't like."

"For heaven's sake, now, Martha," Sister Miriam was saying, smiling down at me as if she were my older sister. "Whatever you do, don't *over*do it. I'm not telling you to turn into a Pollyanna. Just a little more . . . softness, hm?

Another pitch like Nony's. *"Soften up, Martha. You're so hard on people."* So charity means being soft, I thought. Soft in the head. Truth is hard. Like a lot of girls at Marymound Academy are birdbrains.

As Sister Miriam turned and walked away from me and across the front of the classroom to the door, I picked up my books and stood up to go to my Home Room. I thought the conference was over. But she was leaning her back against the door, blocking my path, her hands hidden under her scapular.

"Can't wait to get out of here, huh, Martha?" she said mysteriously. "Sit down for a minute. They can wait." She leaned hard against the door as another girl tried to open it. The first bell had just rung and I could hear a lot of voices out in the hall.

"Have you ever thought you might have a vocation?" She smiled. "A vocation to the religious life?"

"Uh . . . No." She was looking right through me, as if she could see my soul, as if she knew I was lying.

I had thought of it. The last few times I'd been to the Cloisters. For a museum, it had a very romantic personality. I didn't want to know which parts were fake and which ones were actually from the Middle Ages. I wanted the whole place to be from a time when angels smiled and the Blessed Mother looked like a great woman.

Sister Miriam pushed her index finger under her headpiece and rubbed the deep crease on her forehead. I caught a quick glimpse of some black hair. "You ought to think about it," she said. "I think you'd make a good religious."

How the hell can you say something so personal when you don't know me from a hole in the wall, I wanted to say but didn't. When you just got finished telling me what a stinking little bitch I am. I worshiped her, but she was making me squirm.

"Why do you think I have a— Why do you think what you just said?" I asked. Talking to her alone made me so uneasy I couldn't even put a sentence together.

"It's my intuition. There's a certain look. I've spotted it before. You've got it, that's all. You hate the idea now. But you'll change."

"I've never gotten along with nuns. It's a ridiculous idea."

"Oh neither did I when I was your age." She laughed. "But even that—getting along with the ones who bore you stiff— becomes part of the adventure. If you live your vows, you'll be surprised. Religious life can be a life of passionate intensity."

As usual her finale was poetry.

Very slowly she recited. "She is a garden enclosed, my sister, my promised bride; a garden enclosed, a sealed fountain."

She opened the classroom door for me. "That's from the Song of Songs," she said. As I passed in front of her, she said in the way a mother would give orders to her kid about how to behave at a birthday party, "Remember now: no phony smiles . . . Just be yourself. And think about what I said. After the first two years it's a wonderful life." The kids at the front of the line waiting to get into the classroom heard her. I wanted to die.

At the end of the corridor I met Maria Mannion.

"What a brown nose you've turned into, Girlinghausen. Coming to school early to suck up to that phony nun. Next you'll be joining up."

The day we got our Senior rings we christened them in beer in Yorkville. Ernest, our favorite waiter, gave us a round on the Brew House. Most of us had made it through Fat Josie's gauntlet to Senior year. Except for Mannion. Josie had stopped her on the marble staircase the first day back to school.

"What do you think you're doing here, Miss Mannion? You failed three Regents: English, History, and French."

"But I went to summer school," Mannion said. "I passed everything."

"I told you on the telephone last June. It didn't matter whether you went to summer school or not. You're finished here, out. Try Delehanty downtown."

"Dele-*who?*" Mannion screamed. "What the hell is that? An eating place?"

She came to our Ring Day celebration in the uniform of Our Lady of the Miraculous Medal Academy. "Daddy said, 'This is the last and I mean the *last* goddamn principal in the Archdiocese I'll bribe for you, Maria. If Miraculous Medal won't keep you, you can either get married or go to Katherine Gibbs, but I am washing my hands.' "

I left the Brew House early because I had to go to Gleason's Funeral Parlor out in Flushing. Senior Ring Day was also the last day of Michael Quirk's wake. The boy who wanted to be a sailor back in the seventh grade and spit in all the great rivers in the world only got as far as Nebraska. After Regis threw him out for failing Latin, his father bought him a motorcycle.

Quirk was crossing the country when a truck in front of him
backfired and turned him into a torch.

I shared the *prie-dieu* that was placed beside his coffin with
Monica Sheridan who was engaged to be married the day after
her graduation from Flushing High School. By the time the
wake was over, half our class from St. Francis' had been in and
out of Gleason's. Monica Sheridan clung to her hunky fiancé,
an old altar boy from Nony's class. Rosie O'Grady's mother
was there telling everyone that though Rosie was now known
as Sister Mary Angelica she was still "the same old Rosie."
(She wasn't. She sent me goppy Christmas cards with the only
message "May Jesus and Mary bless you on this holy feast".)
Sister Jane Agnes, still the same old iron-eyed bitch, showed
up in a flock of nuns and flapped past us with a disapproving
smile. Bold Robert Emmet Quinn was the only boy in the
lobby of the funeral parlor who didn't crush out his cigarette
on sight of her. It was a hell of a place to have a class reunion,
over Quirk's dead body.

When Robert Emmet Quinn knelt down next to me at the
funeral Mass the next morning, I didn't curl my lip at him or
move to another part of the pew. How could anyone keep up
a childish game of pretending to despise someone you liked
with a coffin sitting in the middle aisle? Monsignor McGoffey
sprinkled the coffin with holy water and I read the psalm he
recited in Latin.

> *If Thou, O Lord, shalt observe iniquities,*
> *Lord, who shall endure it?*

Holding grudges felt as heavy as death. Mr. Quirk was
holding Mrs. Quirk up in the first pew. I thought I heard her
sobbing.

Monsignor McGoffey was as fake as Ed Sullivan when he played the good-time Charlie role at parish card parties, but at Quirk's funeral, he acted like a plain priest for a change. He said the Mass and read the Gospel as if he were performing the most important actions on earth. Even though the baritone's "Dies Irae" thundering down from the choir loft made it sound like death was the last word, I think Monsignor's manner or the Mass or just the grace of God made the Quirks believe what the Gospel said—that their son had not died forever, that Michael Quirk, though dead and charred and mangled, Michael Quirk would rise again. By the end of the Mass, Mrs. Quirk was calm and she and Mr. Quirk were standing straight.

Bold Robert Emmet and I walked home from the funeral together. I noticed he shaved now. His shoulders were so broad, I couldn't think of anything much to talk about.

"Where are you going to college?"

"I don't know. Maybe Fordham."

From the silence that followed it was obvious he didn't want to discuss colleges any more than I did.

He was looking my size 7 figure up and down.

"God, Martha. You were the fattest freshman who ever landed on Bear Mountain. What have you done to yourself?"

"I live on black coffee and Luckies."

We turned a corner and walked along the edge of Bowne Park. "There's the scene of the crime," I said. "You know, where we rallied the troops against the Agony."

"What a bust," he said. "Like most insurrections."

All of a sudden three tiny girls, two of them on roller skates came up behind us from out of the park and bumped into Robert. I recognized his little sisters. The smallest one hugged

him around the knees. Most boys his age would say "Get lost"
to a kid sister or brother who caught him talking to a girl.
Robert bent down and gave her a kiss. Then he tightened the
skates of the older two.

"Martha, I'd like you to meet my sisters, Monica and Betsy
and Kathleen. Girls, this is Martha."

He could have been their father he acted so proud of them,
their mother, he seemed so soft. We watched the two older
ones skate into the park and the littlest one was running to
keep up with them and turning to wave back at Robert. He
was beaming at her and he didn't care what anybody thought
of him for it.

The rest of the way home we talked about his sisters. As we
got to my driveway the conversation switched to books. It
turned out we were both halfway through *Madame Bovary* and
we didn't give a damn that it was on the Index.

I wasn't in the house ten minutes when he phoned. "Would
you consider going to the movies this weekend, Skinny?"

I kept my voice very matter-of-fact as I asked my mother for
permission. My heart was pounding. Bold Robert Emmet, the
darlin' of Erin—he and I were a couple again.

Because Fat Josie was driving her mad, Sister Miriam had
gotten a transfer out of the Academy that year. Every few
weeks I went to visit her at her new school. She talked mostly
about her dissertation which was on the poetry of D. H.
Lawrence. I'd read *Women in Love* during biology class the
year before. I wondered more about how a nun could special-
ize in such a sexy writer than I did about the story. Nuns, I'd
heard, were supposed to wrap themselves in sheets while they
took their baths.

Now and then she told me a story about convent life and teasingly said, "You'll find out about that when you enter, right, Martha?" I got her off that track by rambling on about the different colleges I was applying to—Cherry Hill for my parents; Iowa for Irene, who often said she wished she'd known about its writing program when she was at my stage; and Northwestern because I liked the name. (After going through six boxes of college catalogues at the Forty-second Street library, I didn't know one place from another. They all sounded the same.)

One afternoon Sister Miriam asked me if I had a boyfriend. "There's nobody special," I lied. To such a brainy creature I knew I'd sound like an ass if I tried to make conversation about Bold Robert Emmet. And a dusky convent parlor was not the place to talk about the light of my life. I saved the goo for my weekly letters to Irene.

". . . He is Mr. Wonderful, Irene, you would love him, I know. His favorite writer is Graham Greene, he likes all kinds of music, and we've gone out every weekend since we got back together. Our favorite place is Folk City in the Village. One night Bold Robert was actually invited up on stage to teach an Irish folk song to the Chad Mitchell Trio! I have never been so crazy about anybody. He is the only boy I have *ever* known who I can talk about books to. I have had some great crushes before, but usually I get sick of people fast and that goes for girls as well as boys. But this, my dear sister, is The Real Thing!!! . . ."

I did consider the possibility that Robert Emmet was only using me. I was convenient, living across the street from him —he didn't have to spend the middle of the night on the subway after he took me home. And when we said good night

I didn't pull a June Allyson and just offer him a cheek. Maybe I was a fool. Did he brag to his friends about how easy I was? Did he refer to me as an occasion of sin in confession? Oh, well, if he did that was really a compliment, wasn't it? *"She's irresistible, Father."* . . . *"You must give her up, my son." "I can't, I can't."* . . . As long as Bold Robert's purpose of amendment stayed loose, life would continue to be beautiful.

And then over the telephone one week night in April, he invited me to his Senior prom. I knew, once and for all, that my status as his number-one, only girl friend was real. Everyone knows you only invite someone you really care about to your Senior prom.

I went to school early the next morning to tell my victory before the bell rang for first period. In the coat room where there was supposed to be Silence at All Times, I whispered the news to Elizabeth Filippi. She squealed and passed it on to Bunny McCaffery. Bunny said "Congratulations" right out loud. Like Batman, Fat Josie appeared in the doorway.

"I want to see everyone who opened her lips in here in my office at three o'clock."

Dumb Bunny tried to escape. "All I said was 'Congratulations' to Martha because Robert Quinn asked her to his prom."

Half an hour later, Josie interrupted our Religion class. In the morning mail she'd gotten word from a few colleges telling whom they'd accepted and rejected. She read the lists of names and told the rejects they should have studied harder. I got both barrels.

"I was very surprised to learn," she said, "that the College of Cherry Hill has given Miss Girlinghausen back there a scholarship. But when I get through with the letter of recommendation they've asked me for, she'll be lucky if she gets in down the block at Hunter, where anything goes. Your good Catholic colleges want character. She may have high scores on the College Boards. But she has no character. I know she's fooled a few people. Sister Miriam was foolish enough to make her an editor of the paper just because she was good in English. You should hear Miss Girlinghausen's mother trying to defend her down in my office after I've caught her dear daughter disgracing the school. Now I hear a fine boy has invited her to his Senior prom. Take my word for it: if that boy had seen the photographs I have of Miss Scholarship back there behaving like a common tramp, there wouldn't be any Senior prom, I can tell you. When I get finished telling Cherry Hill about her, that will be the end of any scholarship."

She'll never get away with it, I thought. Nony is a class president at Cherry Hill. They'll never believe her little sister is trash. I held my breath, stared up at the crucifix, and said to myself, "I'm going to his prom, I'm going to his prom" over and over again until the old sow shut up.

My mother got home from school before I did and opened my letter from Cherry Hill's Office of Admissions. She was so happy that I kept quiet about not wanting to go there. I knew enough not to mention Fat Josie's threat. My mother would have been on the phone in a second threatening her back. And then the next day at school Josie would come after me again.

All through dinner that night my mother and father talked Cherry Hill, what a good reputation it had, how much it had done for Nony, how friendly and lively the girls were.

"These kids of ours are lucky," my father said. "In our day there weren't any breaks like scholarships."

"We can afford to send her without the scholarship."

"Oh, listen to Mrs. Gotrocks."

They hovered on the edge of a fight about money. We do have it, we don't have it. All of a sudden they were in fighting moods, she because her father had sent her to Teachers' Training School instead of college, he because he'd dropped out of N.Y.U. night school. *"The stink of feet and cigars damn near suffocated me. . . ."*

"It's funny," I said lamely. "I mean, that Cherry Hill is the place I got a scholarship to because I don't really want to go there." I didn't know where I wanted to go.

The dinner table became quiet. They were allies again.

"God, these kids of ours don't know when they're well off. Where *do* you want to go?"

"No, just a minute here. What I want to know, first of all, is what is wrong with Cherry Hill?"

"It's blah."

My mother got up from the table and started clearing. "I don't have to sit here and listen to such nonsense."

"I think Northwestern is a much better school," I said as she disappeared into the kitchen. "I like the name." Once I'd won the Daily Double at Saratoga by picking a horse for its name, Tempestuous.

She came back into the dining room holding the ice cream scoop. We always had ice cream for dessert to celebrate good report cards and scholarships.

"Perhaps you've forgotten the rule: if you live at home you can go anyplace you like. You won't find a better college than

Hunter anywhere in the country."

I did not want to live at home. I'd been their only child long enough. Since Nony had gone away to college, the house had felt like a funeral parlor, the bedroom we'd shared like a tomb.

"You know, what's so great about college anyway?" I said.

They both answered at once: "You're too damn fresh!"

"If you go away to school," she continued, "it must be to a Catholic college. That's final."

Strike Iowa. Strike Northwestern, I thought. Whether I get in or not.

She went back into the kitchen. Through the doorway I saw her rubbing her back, the "lower lumbar region" where she'd had three operations because she'd had three babies. My father stared at the centerpiece as if he was seeing not a bowl of tulips but all the boring roads he'd driven for years selling copper or paper or whatever it was so his daughters could go to college and be somebody. He cleared his throat in the way that meant he was disgusted.

I was disgusting. Seventeen years old and no idea of what I wanted to be, still leeching off my parents . . . They should know Fat Josie has another fight in store for them . . . they'll blow up the school before they'll let her get away with this one . . . they always stick up for me. *"If a nun ever lays a hand on you, I'll go down to that convent and hit her back"* . . . the first place he went after being in bed three months after his heart attack was to the rectory over Sister Ursula's pulling my ear . . . And I sit here and take pot shots at a perfectly decent college that Mother would have given her eye teeth to go to . . . It won't be so bad . . . Bold Robert and I can go to the city on weekends, study together during the week . . .

I helped my mother serve the ice cream and the layer cake she'd made especially for me. "What are Robert Quinn's plans?" she asked.

"I'm not sure. Fordham, I guess." He never seemed to want to talk about colleges.

We began to eat the special dessert. My father put down his fork.

"Let's get this straight: we let you pick your high school and we wound up with that fishwife they call a principal driving us nuts for four years. Your mother and I are picking your college. You're going to Cherry Hill, is that clear?"

"Oh, Daddy," I said. "C'mon. I was only kidding around. The cake is great, Ma."

My mother said the same thing after every play and concert that her three daughters were ever in. "You were the best. Nobody else was nearly as good as you." She said it even if we'd forgotten a few lines or played some wrong notes.

I inherited her habit of thinking that what meant something to me was ipso facto the best of its kind. There was no better English teacher than Sister Miriam. New York was the greatest city in the world. Nobody else had sisters who compared with mine. The night of his Senior prom, it was as plain as the smell of spring—Bold Robert Emmet was perfection.

Instead of the usual white jacket that most boys wore to spring formals, he had on a beige-ish jacket made of the finest purest linen. He was right out of a *New Yorker* ad. He wasn't embarrassed to say "Your dress is beautiful, Martha. It becomes you." Because of his good taste, I didn't have to ruin its simple lines with a fat corsage. He brought me a wristlet of tiny white cymbidiums. He didn't gape at the potted palm trees around the dance floor as if he'd never danced in a big-city hotel before. He didn't drape his arms all over me when we had our picture taken with the other couples at our table. And he tipped the waiters who brought the drinks from the bar without a lot of hullabaloo. The other guys, as each round was served, shouted the length of the table, "Yuh got change of half a dollah down there?"

By the time the band struck up "Good Night, Sweetheart" the frozen daiquiris I'd been guzzling all night had gone to my head. Earlier, during one of the band's intermissions, Robert had asked me out of the blue what I wanted to be, and I'd said "A teacher, I guess." Now as we started dancing the last dance, I stood on tiptoes and accidentally touched his earlobe with my mouth. "You know what I said before?" I whispered, "about being a teacher? Well, it's not true." He had to bend his head down to hear me. "I want to find something I can do with *devotion.* Something I can give my whole mind and heart and soul to." I felt myself floating on rum up to a place where everything was going to be perfect. Maybe someday I will marry you, Bold Robert, I thought. Then he kissed me on the forehead, but lightly, platonically. I sang along with the music. "Good night, Sweetheart, till we meet tomorrow. Good night, Sweetheart . . ."

"Shut up, you're singing off key. You better sober up. We've got a long night ahead of us."

The first question put to promtrotters their first day back at school was "Where did you go afterwards?" After the prom was as sacred as Christmas Eve. To be authentic the all-night ritual had to include going to at least two nightclubs. To be the most perfect night of a girl's life, it had to end with watching the sunrise from the Staten Island Ferry.

"Let's go for a ferry ride," I shouted. "Good Night, Sweetheart" was ending with an explosion of brass.

Like a real gallant, Bold Robert raised my arm into the air and smelled my cymbidiums.

"I made reservations for the ten of us—our whole table— at the Stork Club and the Plaza. Let's play the rest by ear."

There was light in the sky by the time the ten of us left the Plaza. And now to the ferry, I thought. Then I heard eight of us exclaiming like a bunch of tourists over the hansom cabs they saw parked along Central Park South.

"Oh, look!"

"Let's grab one of those!"

"What do you say, Pat?"

"How 'bout a ride through Central Park?"

They ran across the street. That was the end of any ferry ride. We were all in the same party. The ten of us were still to go to a breakfast party out in Bayside.

It was also the end of the hansom cabs. I saw the last one take off as Robert and I sauntered across the street.

"That's pretty rotten," I said. "They just took off and left us stranded."

"We're not stranded."

"But they could've waited for us. Now we have to hang around waiting for them."

"Oh, bitch, bitch, bitch. Take it easy, Martha. This is my last—"

I didn't care for his tone of voice. "Your last what?"

"Nothing. Forget I said that."

"I'm freezing."

"It's windy here," he said. He picked me up, as if I was as light as one of his little sisters and carried me back to the square opposite the front entrance to the Plaza. Then he put his gorgeous linen jacket around my shoulders.

We sat down to wait on the steps under a fountain of some goddess, Diana or Venus or somebody. The water in the fountain had been shut off.

I looked at his watch. "It's almost five in the morning."

"Today is Pentecost Sunday," he said.

We both looked up at the Plaza at once.

"It's the most beautiful building in the city, I think."

"The view from the top rooms facing the park must be fantastic. I wonder which room it was in *The Great Gatsby,* at the end where they all got smashed and had it out."

"Speaking of coming clean . . ." Bold Robert Emmet took my hand in his. His fingers were limp.

"I'm not going to Fordham."

"You never said you were." I took my hand away. I can't stand the feel of limp fingers.

"No, I know. I've got to tell you something." He lit a cigarette. "I know this may come as a surprise. I'm entering the Jesuits."

"Oh, my God. Are you kidding?"

"Before . . . when I said 'This is my last—' That's what I meant. This is my last dance."

"Oh . . . your last *dance* . . . Jesus, that's really something. You, a priest."

A goddamn priest. I shouldn't have been surprised. The brains always went into seminaries and convents. Look at Sister Miriam.

"Are you surprised?" He looked sheepish.

"Sort of. But not really. It's supposed to be the best thing a person can be, right?" In my heart of hearts I thought he was committing suicide, a gray, halfhearted suicide. I had contemplated the same kind. *She is a garden enclosed; my sister, my promised bride.*

"That's it exactly," he said quickly. "It's the best, the most significant thing I can do. Most people waste their lives doing things that aren't very important."

He was full of the priesthood already and it made me sick. We were never going to see one another again and he could sit there beneath the fountain and sound exhilarated. I was going to look like such a fool once this news was out. *"Some hot romance those two must have had."* I should have guessed. I remembered how he'd concentrated so intently on his missal at Quirk's funeral.

Then I heard the slow trot of the hansom cabs returning down Central Park South.

"Does anyone we're with tonight know?"

"No. Outside of my family, you're the only one. I thought you had a right to know first."

I acted very sweet to him on the way home in the cab and at the breakfast party in Bayside. But when he tried to kiss me on my front stoop, I turned away.

"You can't have your cake and eat it too," I said.

Bold Robert Emmet did not die with a smile. He had the gall to look hurt.

I saved a few petals from the wristlet of cymbidiums he'd given me. I pressed them inside my missal between the pages of the Mass for Pentecost Sunday, right under the "Alleluia, Alleluia, Send forth Thy Spirit, and they shall be created and Thou shalt renew the face of the earth, Alleluia." He left for the seminary eight weeks later. Alleluia, my ass.

4

"Good afternoon, my dear Freshmen. You look very frightened. You should be frightened. If I manage to get nothing else across this afternoon but the idea that you are about to embark on a long and laborious journey my time behind this lectern will not have been spent in vain.

"First of all, let me share with you a few of the facts of life behind Cherry Hill as a community of scholars. These are facts that we in our Dean's Office live and breathe but ones that our Freshmen know little of. The first fact is this: no one, or almost no one, at Cherry Hill gets A. A means perfect. Do *not* expect A's. Let me say it again. Do *not* expect A's. Or, for that matter, B's. C is the average grade of the average student at Cherry Hill. I don't care if you got all nineties in high school. I don't care if you have always been at the very top of your honor roll. By the end of the first exam period you will know what I am talking about today: the intellectual standards at Cherry Hill College are like mountain peaks. Most of our CHC students dwell in the valleys. Some do ascend. And yes, a few, a *very* few reach the summit. But most of you will have all you can do to exist, to stay alive in the valley. And if I may extend my metaphor a bit further, let me warn you about life in the valley. It is a tough and challenging milieu. There are periodic floods called midterm examinations, hurricanes called term papers, and tornadoes in the form of final examinations. So be vigilant, valley dwellers. Pursue excellence. Strive to develop your God-given potential. By the end of your four-year journey you will know in what way you are meant to use that potential, whether it be a vocation to the religious, married, or single state. Always remember: you do not make this journey of the intellectual life alone. CHC is blessed with a fine faculty—this year, just last Friday afternoon, in fact, I hired number ninety-four. We also have on our staff a dedicated counselor and beloved chaplain, Father James O'Rourke. And though the duties of an Academic Dean are many, my door, too, is always open. For if you look at the crest on the pockets of your Senior sisters' blazers you will read the Latin word *Serviam.* Those of you who studied Latin in high school can translate. *Serviam* means 'I will serve.' It is the motto of each and every one of us at Cherry Hill—of the administration, the alumnae, the faculty, and, we hope, the student body. *Serviam* is a synonym for the CHC experience. Your goal from your first day on campus to your last is to develop your fullest potential, intellectual and spiritual. At Cherry Hill we are also involved with morality, which, as you will learn in Ethics class, concerns the choice between right and wrong. The most important purpose of your intellectual, spiritual, and moral development is that you make yourselves fit to serve the needs of others: to think and live and pray "Serviam" long after your Senior blazers have been put into moth balls. Of course, there will be among you a few crackpots or oddballs, if I may use the vernacular. Do not let them distract you. Eventually they will fall by the wayside. They always do.

"May I close on a personal note? In this morning's mail I received a letter from a loyal alumna who is also a dear friend. Here is part of what she has to say: 'You know, Mother Aquin, when I try to tell my youngest granddaughter, Peggy, about Cherry Hill, about what makes it such a unique and challenging institution I find I can't explain it to her. All I can say is "Peggy, honey, there is something special about a Cherry Hill girl. You can point your finger at her every time." '

"My dear Freshmen, as you begin your intellectual career at Cherry Hill, may I welcome you to campus, may I wish you luck, and may I remind you—there is something special about a Cherry Hill girl. You can point your finger at her every time. Good afternoon."

"Come to Cherry Hill College in beautiful suburban Westchester, only fifty minutes from Broadway and all the cultural advantages of New York City" read the ad in the Education section of *The New York Times.* The ad was a lie. The city was off limits Monday through Friday. To go to the city over the weekend you had to "sign out" with Mother Amandine, the Prefect of Discipline. Signing out meant getting written permission forty-eight hours in advance of your time of departure on the New York Central. This rule did not irritate most Cherry Hill girls. You could point your finger at them on Saturday afternoons ambling along the main street of Cherry

Hill, in and out of Ella's Card Shoppe, Dunkin' Donuts, and Bloomingdales.

"You never told me you can't even go to the goddamn city without a pass from the warden. They ought to have a sign on the main gate—'Abandon the world, ye who enter here.' Jesus, Nony. What a place."

"Oh, calm down. It's like everything else at Cherry Hill. There are good teachers and fools, rules that make sense and stupid rules. If we were allowed to go to the city on weekdays there'd be some people who'd never open a book. If smoking were permitted in the dorms, the insurance rates would go up and so would the tuition. I admit Mother Aquin is all you say —though even she has her good qualities. Frankly, there are so many people at Cherry Hill who are nothing but good it's hard to get too excited about those who fall short. Martha, you've got to see both sides of things, of people, of Cherry Hill, or you're going to be very unhappy. If you spend all your time knocking the place—nit-picking—you're going to miss a lot of good things you could be right at the center of."

Oh, no, 'twas the truth in her eyes ever shining that made me love Nony . . .

I'd gone to Nony's room to borrow her milk of magnesia. After one week at Cherry Hill I'd sat down at my desk and eaten two pounds of chicken corn candy. (You couldn't smoke anyplace on campus except in the Smoker, which closed at 6:00 P.M.) The candy didn't make me feel any sicker than the constant sound of smiling girls' voices—"Hi, there! I'm Kathy O'Brien from Westport." I stared at the "Serviam" on Nony's Senior blazer. I'd slog through the four years. I couldn't think of anything else to do. At least by the time the Prefect of Discipline handed me my blazer I'd have found out what I was going to do with my life.

"Which one do you like, darling? You can have any one you want. Nothing is too good for Mrs. Michael Tapia. Remember the old saying—a diamond is forever."

"I don't know. Something simple. You pick it." We had wandered into the Diamond Center on Forty-seventh Street after a Saturday matinee at the opera.

"That one there, the sort of pear-shaped thing with the little chips around the diamond, that one is very beautiful. Is that what you call a Tiffany setting?"

"I don't know. I don't know much about settings." He had tried to hold my hand during the opera, while Pagliacci's heart was breaking.

He hugged me. "Mrs. Michael Tapia." He sighed. "Two years from this June I'll give you a ring. Provided everything works out at med school. Two years after that we can get married. Let's have the wedding in June too. You'll make a beautiful June bride."

She is a garden enclosed; my sister, my promised bride . . . I'd told him I'd marry him though I didn't know him very well. It was his name I liked the night I met him at the Cherry Hill Fall Mixer. *"Not every man has flowers in his house at slow, sad Michaelmas . . ."*

He turned to look again at the diamonds and his own reflection in the window of the Futurama Jewelry Exchange. I watched him and saw myself arranging long-stem red roses anniversary after anniversary, my pear-shaped diamond flashing across a dim empty living room somewhere in Connecticut.

Michael was smiling as he squinted at the price tags on the rings. Over Christmas vacation I'd thought it might happen we'd sleep together. We were practically engaged. Instead he took me here and there to meet his relatives and one day we drove out on Long Island to see the church where he'd made his First Communion. "What made you decide to be a doctor?" I asked him as he led me toward the outdoor shrine to St. Anthony. He wanted to be a doctor because it was a very secure line of work and because if his brother could get through med school, then by gosh, he could.

He was in a trance staring at the diamonds. I ran across Forty-seventh Street and hid for two hours in the Gotham Book Mart. It was a miracle that I realized before it was too late that life with him would be death.

The same night that Cherry Hill gave Fulton Lewis a hero's welcome, my mother phoned about Irene and Steve. After Fulton Lewis warned about Communist infiltration in the National Students' Association, a good half of the CHC audience stood and cheered. Then Fulton Lewis showed a movie put out by HUAC in which college students in California were seen being hosed off the steps of the state capitol by state troopers. The Cherry Hill girls clapped for the California cops. Up in the balcony two CHC philosophy teachers, scowling and puffing their pipes, did not applaud. They were the same two who had frowned and done nothing three years before when their colleague had gotten the ax for shouting down the McCarthyite at the "Talk Without Chalk." Amidst all the cheering I did not have the nerve to boo. I tiptoed out early and tried not to make a sound when I closed the door to the gym behind me. I heard the phone ringing and then my call bell as I walked into the dormitory.

"Well, *we* had quite a weekend," Mother began. "I don't like to disturb your studies, Martha, but I feel it's only right you should know."

"What's happened?"

"Irene telephoned us a little after two o'clock on Saturday. I'd just come in from the Safeway and Daddy was listening to the opera. I got on and Irene said, 'Mother, could you and Daddy come up?' I asked what was wrong, but all she would say was 'Please. Just come.' Well, you know Irene has always been given to exaggeration, so first I put away the groceries and had a sandwich and after I read the mail and changed my clothes and looked for some old construction paper I'd been saving for the children since last Valentine's Day, we got in the car and drove up there. On the way we stopped for vegetables and I said to Daddy, 'Do you think anything's really wrong?' "

"Well, is there? What's up?"

"We weren't in the house ten seconds and I had my answer. Steve came out on the landing looking like the devil and told us to get out of his house or he'd throw us out. For a minute I got frightened. I always have to keep Daddy's heart in mind. But Daddy—" Mother laughed and went on—"Daddy told Steve he had a baseball bat in the trunk of the car and he'd bash Steve's skull in if he tried to stop us from going upstairs to see Irene."

"Were the children there?"

"Oh, yes. They watched the whole thing from the third floor landing, all of them half dressed, Paul without even a diaper on him. There's very little those children have not seen. We found Irene, that beautiful girl, lying in bed with a fever and her face swollen from weeping. I had to sit down on the edge of the bed—I thought I might black out. Do you know that that bastard she's married to has been abusing her since nineteen fifty?"

"My God. What do you mean?"

"What do I mean? He's been *beating* her, that's what I mean!" She hasn't told us because of Daddy's heart. But I know her real reason—we pleaded with her not to marry him, I warned her he was no good. I don't blame her for wanting to save her pride. What girl wants to have to face her parents and say, 'Mother, you were right. Everything you ever said about him turned out to be true.' "

"Is there going to be a divorce?"

"Oh, there was no talk of *that.* Though, on the way home, Daddy did say she should dump him. They've been seeing their priest, a Father Dumfrey or Humphrey, some name like that, from Saint Dominic's, who, Irene says, had been having a good effect on Steve until Saturday. To give him his due, he's been under a lot of pressure at work since they moved back from Pennsylvania. . . . I don't want you to worry about this, Martha, there's no need for it to interfere with your school work because there's nothing you or anybody can do except say your prayers. . . . What kind of a weekend did you have?"

Back in high school Sister Miriam had read us a short story by Ernest Hemingway called "A Clean, Well-Lighted Place." She said its ending was famous. "Our nada who art in nada, nada be thy name." I had not thought about the story or its ending since the afternoon Sister Miriam read it to our English class. But the night that followed my mother's phone call about Irene and Steve I thought about it. I considered for the first time that the character who said "It was all a nothing" might be right.

I remembered Irene rocking her children in Pennsylvania, Irene shoveling out the driveway after the blizzard of '47, trying to teach me to swim summers in Saugerties. Each memory of her was followed by an image of Irene now—being beaten. Maybe right then in the middle of the night while the six children slept or lay awake in their cribs listening. Children could always hear what was going on downstairs, scuffling, glass breaking, their mother's sobbing. *"There's nothing you can do for her except say your prayers."* Hail nothing. I remembered the way Irene always looked so reverent coming back from Communion. When she was fifteen she announced she wanted to join the Little Sisters of the Sick Poor. Nony and I teased her about the Big Sisters of the Healthy Wealthy. Nony said Irene was the holiest in the family. Suffering was supposed to come to holy people, the ones God loves best. The starving and the tortured are really God's closest friends. Or were they the irrefutable evidence that it was all a nothing? "He's been *beating* her, that's what!" My mother's voice, unchastened, echoed in my head all night long. At 5:00 A.M. I escaped the voice and my roommate's snoring. I put on the academic gown we had to wear to chapel and walked across the dark campus to the Nuns' Mass.

Only a handful of students ever got up early enough for the Nuns' Mass. We sat in the last pew. I liked the cold Gothic chapel with the rough white plaster walls and the shuddering sound of the nuns' serge habits as they swept down the aisles and into the pews. *"Mea culpa, mea culpa, mea maxima culpa!"* Father O'Rourke pronounced the words of the Confiteor with conviction. *"Renie did it, Renie did it, Renie did it!"* Time after time I had tattled on Irene, and weekend after weekend she got thrashed because of me. I helped push her from the frying pan into the fire. Father O'Rourke moved slowly leftward to the Gospel side of the altar. What would he say if he got Steve in confession? *"Go and beat her no more."* I watched the nuns incline toward the altar at the tense moment of the Consecration. They looked as if they'd stake their lives on there being a God up there. How could it all be a nothing with nuns on their knees at dawn, day in and day out, laying down their lives for others.

I decided to get up every morning at five and go to the Nuns' Mass. I couldn't think of anything else to do for Irene. Once daylight came, I wished she'd get a divorce.

The Pig Pool, a game that Cherry Hill girls could play with any men's college, was the brain child of Suzy Daly from Larchmont. The players from Cherry Hill, and, say, Iona College, signed up for blind dates for the Saturday Night Mixer and put twenty-five cents in the kitty. The prize money was awarded to the girl and boy who everyone agreed had drawn the ugliest date—the Pig—from the pool of blind dates.

For once I did not draw an Accounting major who after a few cups of cherry punch dug out of his wallet the letter he'd written to the *Daily News* and gotten published by golly. My blind date turned out to be an American Indian. He was born in South Dakota, grew up in Canada, had worked in Chicago, and was now paying his way through night school by working on the construction of the Verrazano Bridge in New York harbor.

He didn't want to talk about what it was like to work on the world's longest bridge. Places interested him: the Black Hills, the Snake River Valley, San Francisco. He hated Chicago. "A place for savages," he called it. "My mother's still stuck out there. As soon as I can, I'm bringing her to New York."

Suzy Daly and her fiancé, the nephew of a New Jersey Supreme Court judge, brushed past us and I felt Suzy poke me in the back.

Distracted, I forgot about places and asked Frank if he had any brothers or sisters.

"My father died of alcohol poisoning in the Greyhound Bus Station in Chicago, my brother is in jail in Chicago. I'm going to make it."

Back in the dorm, in Suzy Daly's room, it was unanimous. "You win, Girlinghausen, hands down. The Pig Pool is yours."

Everyone howled. Suzy threw me the prize money, but I said no thanks, who needs a $7.25 kitty? I went back to my room and hid.

. . . You see, my dear friend, I am not going to enter the Carmelites as soon as I had hoped. The Church is changing so much since the election of Pope John. It seems the monastery is adopting a new admissions policy. A candidate for the religious life must have some higher education (a college degree, if possible) before entering. I see the wisdom of this, but the wait is very hard to bear. I have wanted to give myself completely to the Mystical Body of Christ for so long now. Also I hate St. John's so much, I cannot tell you. I worry that by the time I am accepted at the monastery I will have lost my faith. Ever since we studied St. Thomas's five proofs for the existence of God in Theology class, I have been greatly upset. You see, I can disprove every one of them. Please pray for me. I'm sorry we couldn't get together over Thanksgiving. Did you happen to watch Edward R. Murrow's documentary on the migrant workers? It so upset me I had to stay away from St. John's for a week. All they care about here is going to Bermuda over Easter vacation.

Your loving friend,
Nina

P.S. I took your advice and got *Kristin Lavransdatter* out of the library, but I just don't like novels. For my spiritual reading this month I'm reading a new biography of Teresa of Avila. What a great woman and saint she was! Yes, we also studied "The Love Song of J. Alfred Prufrock" but in Moral Philosophy class, not in English. Our Professor used it as an example of the

fear of existential commitment. I hope when we see one another I can straighten you out about philosophy. It is not as dull
as you say, if it is taught well, though I agree that metaphysics
can be very boring, particularly if you are interested in existen-
tialism. You must read *I and Thou* by Martin Buber. I'll lend
you my copy when we meet at Christmas. No, I have never
heard of Simone Weil.

We had to be back on campus by 8:00 P.M. the Sunday night
at the end of the Christmas vacation. That was the noisiest
night of the year in the Seniors' dormitory. Screams broke out
in the shower room, the phone room, up and down corridors,
as one Senior after another turned up wearing the diamond
gotten at Midnight Mass or on New Year's Eve.

"Judy! Oh, JUDY! Congratulations!"

"Oh, no!"

"Oh, my God, not you too! When? I mean when's the
wedding?"

"Eileen got hers too!"

"Oh, I'm so *happy* for you."

"Oh, my God, look at *this* one!"

"Mary LOU!"

For some Seniors, that night was a deadline as important in
its way as the date for submitting the Thesis required for
graduation. If you were going to have a big June wedding, you
had to come back from the Christmas holidays engaged. No
one at Cherry Hill said you had to march from graduation into
matrimony. But a June wedding was a real answer to the

question, "What are your plans after graduation?" And the longer you thought about graduating unengaged and going back to Syracuse or Flushing and living with your parents again, the more ideal a June wedding looked. It was a final solution of sorts. The prospect of growing old alone, contemplated from a narrow cot in the Senior dormitory, easily became the chronic nightmare of many a Senior year.

Nony made the deadline. On December 28, the Feast of the Holy Innocents, which, unknown to her fiancé, was also Irene and Steve's eighth wedding anniversary, she got her ring.

Her bridegroom-to-be was a West Pointer who looked as movie-star gorgeous in his uniform as Tyrone Power in *The Long Gray Line.* Lieutenant Phil was also tone deaf.

"Nope. I can't even manage 'The Star-Spangled Banner,' which, let me tell you, was a very tough handicap at the Point."

Daddy's only reservation about Phil was that he was military. "It's a good thing Grandma isn't around for this. She left Germany to get away from Bismarck and she never stopped harping on the military. She despised them."

My mother was charmed by Phil and enthusiastically began planning a big wedding. Once in a while she did look up from her lists of Guests for the Showers, Guests for the Church, and Seating Plan for the Reception and say, "One thing does disturb me about Nony and Phil. I wish he knew something about music. If only he could sing a little. Nancy could carry a tune in the bassinet. It's so important for a husband and wife to have some common interests. Though Irene and Steve always had their heads together over the same book and that doesn't seem to have taken them very far, so who knows? . . ."

One Sunday afternoon a few weeks before the wedding, Nony was playing "Poor Wandering One" on the piano and Phil was standing behind her trying to sing along. He was ruining the song. I was lying on the sofa paging through the *Times* and thinking, Why don't you shut up and let her sing, you tone-deaf jerk. But Phil was an amiable relief from Steve who had snarled his way to the altar with Irene. He was even amiable about my mother's burnt zucchini. I watched him massaging Nony's back while she played and sang and he sort of moaned. At the end of the song, Phil turned toward me and bowed.

"Boo!" I yelled. I fired the *Times Magazine* across the living room at him. *"Siss-ss-ss, siss-ss-ss!"* Why not? His singing stunk. He wasn't good enough for Nony. He probably thought Mendelssohn was a goddamn general.

Phil blushed. "Aw, c'mon. At least give a guy a break for tryin'," he said, with forced humor. He hadn't liked being booed.

The day Nony told me she was going to marry Phil I'd said, "I always thought you'd be a nun." "I did too," she said.

Now she turned around on the piano bench and glared at me. "I must apologize for Martha's exceedingly bad manners," she said. "You were doing beautifully, Phil." She turned back to the keyboard and raced hell-bent through "The Minute Waltz."

Phil rested his hand on her shoulder while she played. She had to ask me to be their maid of honor. I was her sister. I watched their two backs. She was his promised bride; his garden enclosed. It was hard to get used to, her being his. Until she went away to Cherry Hill, for fifteen years she'd always been in the other twin bed, across from me at the dinner table, next to me in the back seat of the car, practicing the guitar all the way up to New Hampshire over summer vacations . . . I'd taken her for granted.

The June night she left for good—she tossed her white orchids into the lobby of bridesmaids at the Garden City Hotel, kissed Mother and Daddy good-bye, and ran through the rice to a cab. I got so smashed the furniture in the bedroom turned into fixtures on a carrousel. Nony's empty bed went faster and faster around the mirror and across the ceiling and I thought, She's not gone, she's right there sitting up in bed, home from Cherry Hill for the weekend, telling me about Professor Hill and what a great play *Come Back Little Sheba* is and the two of us laughing about the dopes in her Novel Seminar. *Can you believe that most of them preferred Amelia to Becky Sharp—they loved Amelia and downright hated Becky Sharp!* . . .

The morning after Nony's wedding, her bed was still empty and I swore off stingers for life.

The oral part of the exam for a New York City license to teach high school English had consisted of a gnome in a dark room asking "Now, uh, Miss, uh, Girling . . . how . . . Girl . . . Miss Girling, the question is how would you go about teaching *Romeo and Juliet* to a class of nonreaders in Harlem? Take your time, you have five minutes." The written part I'd heard was read only for grammatical errors so I answered the essay questions on English literature with complete sentences like, "Jonathan Swift believed that Pepsi-Cola hit the spot; Jane Austen, however, affirmed in novel after novel that Lucky Strike means fine tobacco." I received my license in the mail a few months after the exam. My mother got on the phone to my grandmother. "Martha's license came, and now she's all set. As Dad said to me in nineteen twenty-two, when I got my license, you could go farther and do worse."

I took the license off the mantel and tore it up.

"Spoiled brat," said my good self. "The Board of Education got Mother and Daddy through the Depression."

"Does that mean I have to lay down my life for it?" thought the spoiled brat.

"Greater love than this no man hath that he lay down his life for his friend." That was the inscription on the reredos in the Cherry Hill chapel.

My last Christmas vacation as a Cherry Hill girl, I had gone to Washington for an interview with the Peace Corps. On my application I said I was interested in the Peace Corps because I wanted "to help 'build the earth' in the words of Teilhard de Chardin. 'For here on earth God's work must surely be our own,' as President Kennedy said in his Inaugural Address." Nony's husband Phil, who was assigned to the Pentagon, arranged the interview through a friend of his.

"What would you do," the friend of Phil's friend asked, "if you were in Africa, say, on assignment, teaching English, and it turned out you hated it. Hated the job, hated the people, the place, absolutely hated your boss. What would you do?"

"I guess I'd quit," I said.

"Quit?" he snapped. "Never! That would be vocational
suicide. The Peace Corps is a career. If you're lucky, it could
turn out to be a steppingstone to a very solid career in govern-
ment."

"Your friend's friend is an asshole," I told Phil over a
fourth martini that night.

"With a mouth like yours you ought to join the Army,"
Nony said.

"That's my loyal Army wife," Phil said amiably. "Despite
your nasty mouth, little sister, let me tell you two girls what
I'll do—I'll put the Tiger to bed so Nony can have the night
off to drive you to the airport. I'd love to hear more of your
charming comments over breakfast, little sister, but we realize
Gotham calls!"

"What *are* you going to do after graduation?" Nony
sounded critical, as if I should have made up my mind by this
late date in Senior year.

"I'm not moving back to Flushing."

"Doesn't the Guidance Office do career counseling anymore? I got three teaching offers through them."

The clock on her dashboard said we had seven minutes to
get to the last shuttle flight out of Washington.

"They're a half-assed bunch. Last semester they ran a
weekly series of panels on careers at class meeting. All these
successful alumnae showed up to give a spiel on how fulfilling
it is to be a buyer for Bloomingdales and a gossip columnist
on the Bridgeport *Gazette.* I tried to keep an open mind,
Nony, to see both sides. I know there's nothing wrong with

pushing Waterford glass for Bloomingdales. But I don't want a job. I want a great big commitment."

Nony was crisscrossing lanes, cutting off taxis. I thought she wasn't even listening to me. In my martini haze I'd been addressing myself to the blinking red light on top of the Washington Monument.

"Martha, if you want a total commitment—a vocation—and there is no one on the horizon you have in mind to marry, you know as well as I do where you find that."

She had been listening. She swerved into the taxi lane and stopped outside the blue neon wings of Eastern Airlines.

"You've never been one to shy away from a risk. I'm counting on you to fly high," she said.

By the time I was a Senior and the noisiest night of the year exploded in the dormitory, I knew what I was going to do with my life. Like Nony three years earlier, I made the deadline. As I hurried into the Senior dormitory that cold Sunday night at the end of Christmas vacation, I met my old roommate Mary Ellen Butts.

"How was the interview in Washington?" she asked.

"The guy who interviewed me was a bunny rabbit. I'm not joining the Peace Corps."

Mary Ellen stopped at the door of the phone room to check the bulletin board. "Better hurry up and make up your mind," she said. "Time is running out. I had four interviews and three job offers over vacation. All teaching third grade. Now if those offers had been three different men down on their knees pleading, 'Mary Ellen, darling, please marry me, Mary Ellen,' wouldn't I be the star of the dormitory tonight!"

I smiled and scanned the names on the phone messages pinned to the bulletin board. There was one for me from a person I liked very much, a boy from Oregon. He might make me reconsider, I thought, and threw the message in the waste-paper basket. I had made up my mind. I went down to the Senior Smoker and admired the new diamonds, listened to the wedding plans. I felt as exhilarated as the engaged girls looked. For my future was set, too, and it was worthy. It was also radical, total, and insane. I was leaving everything behind on shore—interviews, jobs, the classifieds, Saturday nights, Waterford glass, bunny rabbits. With time's winged chariot rushing at my rear, I had decided to be a nun.

5

The Motherhouse of the community I entered didn't look anything like the Cloisters. The main plant of the Franciscan Sisters of Our Lady of the Woods was a huge Victorian house in a suburb of Columbus, Ohio. I guess it was called the Motherhouse because the Mother General lived there. She had a sort of loge seat in the back of the chapel. From her choir stall that was built on a raised platform she could keep an eye on her community: forty Postulants—the first-year students in black jumpers; the thirty-five Novices—second-year students ("candidates" for vows) in brown habits and white veils; and the Professed—the nuns—all in brown, who had vows of poverty, chastity, and obedience.

In addition to the Motherhouse community, Mother General was in charge of the two hundred nuns who lived on the "missions," the elementary and high schools and one college staffed by the Sisters from the Woods. Mother General decided which nuns would cook, or go for a Master's, or teach first grade at St. Jane's in Boston. In the early sixties she promised a South American Bishop to send some of her Sisters to staff a new mission in the mountains of Peru.

"It's a new direction for our community," Sister Miriam wrote after I'd written to ask her how one went about joining a nunnery.

"Our apostolate has always been teaching. But Peru will mean not only starting a school but also a medical dispensary and a food cooperative. According to Sister Anne Marie (Mother General's companion on her first visit to Peru and the mission's first Superior), the place is so poor it will take a special vocation to last there. We saw the slides of their trip one night at Recreation and you have never in your life seen such pathetically undernourished children."

In the Peace Corps these children would have been the objects of a temporary compassion. As a nun I could go all the way for them, give them everything. Or, for that matter, whatever children I was sent to serve anywhere. With a vow of poverty I would not have to waste any energy worrying about the Board of Education's latest pension plan. Having only one outfit to wear would eliminate wasting time on clothes. The vow of obedience I didn't understand, but it interested me—it made the religious life seem a living paradox: to be free in this world you have to become a slave to the next, to live you must die, or something like that. Chastity, well, Christ was a virgin and His life had passion. The truth was I didn't know what I'd be missing, so I wouldn't waste time worrying about it.

"What are you going to do when you run into Fat Josie?" my father asked cynically. "Or that other one, the monster who tortured Irene down at St. Francis?"

I suspected that at Our Lady of the Woods the Fat Josies were as common as cockroaches in a city hospital. I'd ignore them. They were no more deadly a species than Board of Education drones.

"There's no fool like an old fool," my mother kept saying. "If I'd known she was going to turn around and join them I could have saved my breath on all those trips into Josie's office at Marymound."

"Let's not get sidetracked," my father said glumly. "What I object to most is that it's not natural."

"You get a haircut every month—that's not natural either."

Sister Miriam was as fulfilled as any mother I knew. When I thought of her, Daddy's doubts and my own seemed silly.

"What a marvelous time to belong to the heart of the church," she'd written. "The Council is sending forth great gusts of fresh air which our community has needed for a long time. Last night Mother General's weekly letter was read in the Refectory and it's very reassuring. She is more and more on the side of *aggiornamento.*"

I packed my trunk with the required undershirts, flew United to Columbus, left my Luckies in a cab, and in my new cell changed into the black Postulant's jumper. On the way downstairs to the Refectory I passed Rosie O'Grady—Sister Mary Angelica—coming up. She didn't speak. Dicky Dee, the one who told our seventh grade about sex, offered the grace before meals from a table at the top of the long, red-tiled Refectory. Later, back upstairs in the Common Room where Recreation was held, the Superior—the Mistress of Postulants

—said, "Ordinarily the Professed Sisters do not speak to the Novitiate—to you Postulants and your sister Novices—except on special occasions like tonight." Then the Professed arrived to welcome us to the Woods. They sang "Climb Every Mountain" around an old upright. Rosie took her time coming over to me. When she finally did, she acted disconnected. I told her about Quirk's wake and funeral and she looked at me as if she'd never heard of Quirk or St. Francis Assisi School in Flushing, New York. I asked how she liked teaching. "Teaching is good," she said. "It's good, Sister. But oh, last year I had a terrible class, Sister. They'd been coddled by a lay teacher in fourth. It took me a month to beat them into shape." After the Professed sang "Climb Every Mountain" again and then said good night, we Postulants licked green stamps and pasted them in little books. Five hundred stamp-filled booklets would buy new lawn furniture for the Novitiate garden. Sister Alexa's parents had already donated a tiny kidney-shaped pool for fish and two plastic flamingos to go with it. At nine o'clock a bell rang and we lined up for baths. When my turn came, I locked the door to the tub room behind me, took off my clothes, and turned on the water full force. I did that to drown out the sound. There was nothing to do but kill myself. I was too ashamed to go home, after only four hours in the place. I banged my head against the tub as hard as I could. "You dumb shit," I said out loud. "You dumb shit." My skull held. I tried drowning. But I couldn't make myself stop breathing under water.

All night I made my headache worse by crying over my folly, my impetuosity. Our Lady of the Woods smelled like a rest home, not the Cloisters. I wanted to run away, right then,

but some little worm had made off with my clothes.
The next morning at Mass, a lanky Franciscan read the
Epistle out loud in English and I started to feel better.

As the vine I have brought forth a pleasant odour, and my
flowers are the fruit of honour and riches. I am the mother of
fair love, and of fear, and of knowledge, and of holy hope. In
me is all grace of the way and of the truth, in me is all hope
of life and of virtue. Come over to me, all ye that desire me,
and be filled with my fruits; for my spirit is sweet above honey,
and my inheritance above honey and the honeycomb. . . .

The words from Ecclesiasticus reminded me I'd come to put
an inheritance to work, not to waste time rooting around in
the inevitable stupidities. The Epistle had a nice sound, as
sweet and easy as Duke Ellington.

The food was good, too. The Postulants and Novices did
the cooking. Nothing was wasted. The dishes for over a hundred people got done in twenty minutes because the community (except for Mother General and her Council of six Sisters)
washed and dried them in silence. The mattresses were comfortable and covered with flannel-like Army surplus sheets,
which, along with the habits, underwear, and altar cloths, the
community (except for Mother General) washed, ironed,
sorted, and folded every Saturday. In each person's four-by-
six-cell were a bed, a desk and chair, and a small chest. You
could clean it in less than sixty seconds. We went to bed at ten
and got up at four-thirty. I thought if everyone lived this
simply there would be enough food and space and time for the
whole world.

After Matins, Meditation, and Mass, the day raced by with
housework and classes on the Bible, Gregorian chant, Cate-

chism, the Little Office of the Blessed Virgin Mary, and the Rules of the Community. Silence of the tongue for most of the day and keeping a "guard on the eyes" at all times were the two I liked best. Their purpose was to free you to concentrate on your interior life. They meant you could ignore everybody. Evening Complin at seven-thirty was followed by an hour of Recreation, which ended with a great gong at nine o'clock when Profound Silence began. That meant you weren't to make a sound even if the ghost of Stalin walked through the curtains around your cell.

Once a week we were allowed to write home, no more than four sides of four-inch-by-six-inch paper. All mail—incoming and outgoing—was read by the Superior. "Monastic simplicity makes such great sense," I told my mother, father, and Superior. "I would never have dreamed so many people could live together so efficiently. You should see this place when the mangles in the laundry are going on Saturdays. There's the big mangle for the Professed Sisters' habits and everybody's sheets, and then the little mangles for the collars, sleeves, scapulars, and other parts of the habit. In twelve hours, we put almost two thousand pieces of linen through the mangles and fold another three thousand pieces of underwear. We do the priests' laundry on Fridays."

I wasted my four sides describing Laundry Day because knowing the Superior was looking over my shoulder put a cramp in my mind. Neither did I want to give my mother and father a pain in the ass by running on about the content of my new life that was important to me—the poetry of Ecclesiasticus, the gorgeousness of the chant, and grace.

"In the spirit of Vatican II, I have decided that this year Reception will not be held here at the Motherhouse. The Postulants will receive the habit in the parish church of Saint Rose of Lima."

Some gasps were heard up and down the Postulants' table in the Refectory as Mother General began to read an announcement one Saturday evening after Vespers.

"In this way we can accommodate more of the laity who for the first time since our community settled in Columbus will have a chance to see what a Reception is. Our chapel here at the Woods is simply not big enough for the ecumenical age —for opening up our religious institutions to all of God's People and thus making them relevant to all, laity as well as clergy. Holding Reception at Saint Rose of Lima will be difficult and inconvenient, yes. Breaking with tradition is always difficult."

Mother General coughed and sipped from the glass of water that Dicky Dee proffered.

"But," she continued, wiping her lips with the corner of her large white linen handkerchief, "after much prayer, I feel that this is God's will for our community. And may I remind you that taking Reception to Saint Rose of Lima's offers us the opportunity to honor Saint Rose and to ask her intercession for our mission in Peru? Sister Anne Marie's letters are filled with reports of disease and hungry children. She begs our prayers. Let us make Saint Rose of Lima the special patroness of this year's Reception.

"This is to be a historic Reception for more than one reason. I have just received word that Bishop Stubbs intends to come to Saint Rose's on August twenty-eighth and officiate in person. For the first time in the history of our community our Postulants will receive the habit directly from the hands of our own Bishop. This is indeed an honor for all of us at Our Lady of the Woods."

Till that night, the hoopla over Reception had been reminding me more of *Little Women* than *The Nun in the Modern World*, the book by Cardinal Suenens that our Superior was always raving about. Every day we had three-hour sewing bees in the attic of the Novitiate, during which each Postulant made her own habit. "Oh, Sister Amy, you look adorable!" Sister Dorothy squealed as she helped fit the cap of Amy's headpiece over her brown curls. "I don't think getting ready for a real wedding can be any more exciting than this," Sister Kathleen cried. It was a matter of obedience that the seams and hems of each piece of the habit—the tunic, the big sleeves, the little sleeves, the scapular, the cape, the collar, and the veil—measure three-fourths of one inch exactly. Sometimes the sound of the Postulants' weeping was as loud as the machines' rumble as girls who'd never threaded a needle before they entered the convent sat ripping out their disobedient seams and starting over.

Nony would have done fine in a Novitiate, I thought, after hearing Mother General's news about Reception. Nony had the habit of always looking at both sides of a thing. Surely Mother General's commitment to Vatican II and to the apostolate were as much a part of our Reception as the silly notions heard in the Novitiate Sewing Room.

Sister Amy, the youngest Postulant, was signaling me to

pass her the bowl of macaroni. I saw her face was puffy from crying. That morning in the laundry she'd thrown Dorothy Jackson's padded bras in the dryer by mistake and there'd been hell to pay. A small fire had started and the rubber from the bras had disintegrated and gotten stuck on the Professed Sisters' serge. Poor Amy. Tomorrow she'd be crying again. Sunday was visiting day for the locals. After her parents left, Amy always ran to her cell and collapsed on her cot sobbing.

After twelve hours in the laundry, I wanted more macaroni too. But I passed it up, not only for the intention of the hungry children at the Peru mission. I was thinking ahead to Reception, about how I'd look in the habit. I hated fat nuns.

We had to be accepted for Reception by Mother General. She interviewed each Postulant separately in her office. We were to be prepared to answer questions on the Catechism and the religious life in general. I had to name the corporal works of mercy.

"The corporal works of mercy are seven: to feed the hungry, to give drink to the thirsty, to clothe the naked, to shelter the homeless, to comfort the sick, to visit the imprisoned, to bury the dead."

"All right," Mother General said. Her hands were folded on top of her desk. They were immaculate, like a priest's, no scars, no stains, no paper cuts.

"Now. Why do you wish to receive the religious habit?"

I said the habit offered a kind of freedom, to be more single-minded about whatever our work was. "I do think," I continued, "that maybe sometimes it can interfere with work too."

Her hands disappeared underneath her scapular. "What do
you mean by that?"

"Well, I think sometimes the habit scares people. Also it can
make us seem out of touch with the world."

"We are out of touch with the world," she said. "We're
supposed to be. If I were to change so much as the size of the
hems on the little sleeves, it would upset the old Sisters in the
Infirmary dreadfully. I have to consider them too. Not everything can be renewal and change and relevance."

Mother General exposed one hand, picked up a pen, and on
the piece of paper that had the names of the Postulants she
would interview that week she put a check next to my name.
I guessed I was accepted. I left her office feeling baffled. I'd
expected the woman at the top, the one who controlled the
whole show, who sounded so committed to fresh air in the
church, to have a personality. But she reminded me of a
mummy.

It was ninety-four degrees the day we got the habit. While
Bishop Stubbs rambled on about *aggiornamento* in the diocese
of Columbus, I sat in a pew of St. Rose of Lima church thinking I'll never survive, I'll sweat to death before he's finished.
My body itched all over. My heart pounded with a new cer-
tainty: wearing three layers of wool serge in ninety-four-
degree heat was absurd. No wonder nuns act so bitchy, I
thought. Underneath they're itching and sweating, suffocating
for the love of God, but they can't scratch in public. I heard
the congregation kneeling down behind me. Up in the pulpit
the Bishop turned toward the altar to lead a prayer for the
success of Vatican II. "Do Thou, O Lord, look down upon
us . . ." I knelt and seized my opportunity. Very slowly I

moved one of the hands that was hidden underneath my new scapular and scratched, first my crotch and then both clammy armpits. As the Bishop trailed off the altar and started down the middle aisle, I wanted to run, out of St. Rose of Lima's, and then naked and cool into the nearest birdbath.

I filed out of the pew and got on line behind our new Superior, Sister Alexandrine, the Mistress of Novices. The Schola of six Professed Sisters and two women from St. Rose of Lima parish intoned the "Veni Creator Spiritus," the signal for the Superior to lead her group of newly habited Novices out of the church. Our Reception was the first time that women had been allowed to sing in the church choir, and it was the first time that religious and laity had sung together in the history of the diocese of Columbus. Fresh air was on the way. When the heat wave was almost over was no time to run away. Jackass, I said to myself. You are no hotter in the habit than you would be in a girdle and nylons on the IRT at rush hour.

"Don't worry, Daddy. I didn't cut my hair." Back at the Woods we sat on a bench next to the Novitiate Rose Garden. My father looked sick.

"Oh, I'm so glad to hear that, Martha. I know Daddy is too. The whole length of the Pennsylvania Turnpike I kept praying, 'Please God, let her save me a lock.' You've got the best hair in the family, you know. But I always thought nuns had to cut their hair."

Mother had on the raspberry silk she'd made to wear to Nony and Phil's engagement party. She was also wearing a new single strand of pearls.

"We can cut it off if we want to or we can just leave it short.

Mine's practically the same length it was at Cherry Hill." I
lifted my veil to show them. "Rosie O'Grady's bald as a bat.
She says it's cooler."

"A woman's crowning glory." For a second my father
looked as if he might cry.

"Henry, get up." Mother stood. "What's this one's name
coming toward us, Martha?"

The three of us stood to greet Dicky Dee.

"Well, well, well, the Girlinghosens, I presume. Sit, sit,"
Dicky Dee said, plopping down on the bench next to me
where my mother had been sitting.

I wished she'd get lost. My parents had driven five hundred
miles to visit me. In a few minutes I was going to have to leave
them for noon Rosary and dinner. After that there'd be interruptions for three o'clock Rosary and then Vespers at five.
We'd have less than two hours together.

"What do you think of Sister Elizabeth here?" Dicky Dee
asked my father. "Do you like her new name?"

"She'll always be Martha to me. But it's a nice name."

I liked St. Elizabeth of Hungary. She'd gone all the way,
sold her crown and given everything to the poor. Elizabeth,
the cousin of Mary, had a good story too. In her barren hopeless middle age she conceived and bore the baby John the
Baptist. Elizabeth was proof that desperate lives can bear fruit.
There was hope for Irene, for victims everywhere.

"Are you stationed at the Motherhouse now, Sister?"
Mother asked. She was fanning herself with the program from
Reception. There was no breeze and no shade.

"Yes, I'm home since June, teaching what we call Modern
Catechetics to our Postulants and Novices. That's a fancy

name for the Creed, only now we put it into everyday language. I'm trying to train our Novices," she patted my hand,
"to make what we call the Kerygma—the Good News of
Salvation according to Jesus Christ—intelligible to your average layman."

Across the Rose Garden I saw Dorothy Jackson—Sister
Fides—hurrying toward the back door of the Motherhouse.
She was the community bell ringer that week.

"Our daughter Nancy . . . you had her in the seventh grade
also, I believe, Sister. She is taking a course on, oh, something
to do with the Bible at Catholic University in Washington
where she and her husband are living."

"The Psalms," Daddy said. He mopped the sweat off his
forehead with the piece of paper towel he was never without.

"Oh, Nony wanted to come to your Reception so badly,
Martha. But she promised the boys she'd take them to the
march. Imagine that. Little David, only three years old, and
all excited about a march for civil rights."

"Stuff and nonsense," Dicky Dee said. "This march is nothing more than that faker in the White House trying to get our
minds off the Bay of Pigs. Only a three-year-old would be
fooled into thinking it had something to do with civil rights."

Back in the seventh grade, Dicky Dee's digressions had run
to sex education. In Modern Catechetics they were political.
I already knew she thought the Civil Rights Movement was a
Communist plot, King was a hustler, and Kennedy was a
liberal pinko bad Catholic who had murdered somebody
called Diem, a good Catholic who made regular Retreats at
the Maryknoll Motherhouse whenever he came to visit the
States from wherever he was from.

"Uh, when is the march?" I didn't know how to get them off politics. Mother and Dicky Dee were sniffing each other with contempt. If one of them charged, the suffocating air would start stinking.

Mother was not a woman to be scared off by a right-winger. "The march is today, Martha. I thought you said you'd joined an *active* order," she said with fake joviality. "I thought it would have been nice if besides praying for the success of the Council the Bishop had offered a prayer for the march at Reception. How do you like my new pearls?"

The bell rang for noon Rosary. Dicky Dee and I stood up.

"Shalom!" she said to my parents. That was the word she said on entering and leaving every class in Modern Catechetics. In the Novitiate she was called "Sister Shalom." Rosie O'Grady had told me on Easter that Dicky Dee—"Sister Shalom"—might be elected the next Mother General, she was so popular.

"I'll be back in less than an hour," I said. "We have dinner after Rosary." I walked away quickly, toward the Motherhouse with Dicky Dee. As I passed the St. Francis of Assisi birdbath, I turned to look back at Mother and Daddy.

He was in the Rose Garden smelling what roses were left. She was crouching down behind a trellis trying to take his picture without his noticing. She was facing the sun. When the picture was developed he'd say, "It's overexposed, Gertrude, too much light. The sun should always be behind you when you shoot." Her dress was the same color as the roses. With all the excitement over my Reception, I'd forgotten to congratulate them. The day before had been their wedding anniversary.

When I came back to the bench an hour later, they were gone. I walked around the empty Rose Garden, wiping sweat off my forehead, hiding behind the trellis to reach under my veil to scratch my scalp. I tried to talk to Dorothy Jackson's little sister, but she was too shy to look me in the face. I scared her. I stared at the high iron gates at the end of the main driveway, watching for Mother and Daddy's car. They were never on time for anything—Communions, Graduations, concerts, Mass.

"Where *were* you," I said when they finally came strolling along. My father carried a bulging Macy's shopping bag.

"Take it easy, kid," he said. "Is it a sin to try to cool off in this God-awful climate? I bought my bride here a Tom Collins, and also one for myself, if that's allowed."

"*And* we thought we'd take a look at the state capitol while you were occupied, which was a mistake because we got caught on their one-way system. While we were trying to find a way off it, we did get to hear the news from Washington on the car radio. I wish you could hear the speech that Martin Luther King gave at the Washington Monument. Wasn't it grand, Henry?"

"There's less than an hour left till I have to go to three o'clock Rosary."

"Do you mean to say you have to follow your regular schedule even though you have visitors?" Mother caressed her strand of pearls up and down the way nuns fingered their rosaries.

"Does your boss know we drove five hundred miles with the temperature over ninety all the way?" Daddy put the

Macy's shopping bag on the grass and took off his jacket. "Let's unload this back breaker before the next bell so I don't have to lug the damn thing back to the car still full."

Mother lifted the bag up onto the bench next to her. "I'll go as quickly as I can, Henry. Here, Martha. This is from the Iondola girl who you were friendly with in high school. She apologized for not wrapping it."

It was a paperback of *The Varieties of Religious Experience* by William James. Nina had inscribed it, "To my dearest friend. If it were not for the March, you know I would be with you today. You are always in my prayers."

Mother handed me a package wrapped in white shelf paper. "This is the watch I wrote you about, from the teachers at P.S. 91 . . . and *this,* oh, you'll get a kick out of this. Daddy and I were very touched. That bastard your oldest sister is married to has a nice mother, you have to hand him that. You know she was always very fond of you. Well, here—" She handed me a package wrapped in white tissue paper. "Steve's mother knitted you a black cardigan sweater."

"Mother, I told you we have to hand everything into the community closet. I can't keep it."

"I know, but I couldn't bear to tell her after all that work, so just write her a thank-you note and you don't have to say a word about not being allowed to keep it. Oh, look here, Martha, I brought you the latest pictures of the house with the garden in bloom."

They'd bought an old farmhouse in New Hampshire for their old age. She'd sent me pictures of it under snow, in fall leaves, and overgrown with wildflowers in summer.

"Oh, you would love this house, Martha. There's a river

running through the back yard that we can hear from our bedroom. After a good rain it sounds like a waterfall."

"It starts up in Tuckerman's ravine," Daddy said. "Remember Tuckerman's Ravine? We skirted it the time we climbed Mount Washington. Think the powers that be out here, what do you call her, the General Mother, will ever let you come put your feet in our river?"

"I wouldn't be surprised if she did. The church is changing so fast—in some communities the skirts of the habits are only mid-calf length."

"I wasn't going to mention it—but how do you stand the heat of that thing? For God's sake, Martha, it's wool."

"You get used to it."

"That is what Grandma said to me the day you left. I was having a bad time of it, I must admit. I said, 'Oh, Mother, if anyone had told me Martha would enter a convent! She's the most independent of my three girls.' Grandma said, 'Gertrude, you'll get used to it.' "

Mother was rummaging through the shopping bag as she talked.

"Oh, dammit, Henry. I got newsprint all over my hands. Here, Martha, take these. You wrote you had never heard of Vietnam where Phil is. Daddy saved a few months of the "News of the Week in Review" for you. You *can* read the *Times,* I hope."

"No, no newspapers."

"God in heaven. Where's the map I put in with those papers, Gertrude?"

Mother peered into the still-bulging shopping bag. "There it is; I see it. What a *good* idea, Henry. At least," she said,

putting the map on my lap, "you should be able to have this
—there's nothing wrong with a map of the world, I hope."

"Ah! Here are the things we picked up along the way to
bring back to Irene and Nony. I knew you'd want to see
them."

"Prints from Cleveland, pewter from Philadelphia, seeds
from Burpee . . . Don't you know by now your mother is the
original Lady Bountiful?"

That reminded me of my favorite definition of God: God
is plenitude. Theological abstractions, I knew, did not interest
Mother. How uncomfortable she would have been to hear me
say, *You and your palaver and your overflowing shopping bags and
guest lists and store of plans for the future, you are to me an emblem
of the Creation. It is meet and just we honor you, O Mad Mother
Gertrude.*

As the bell rang for the three o'clock Rosary, I stood up and
dropped William James, the map, and the newspapers back
into her shopping bag. "I know I can't have these, so there's
no point in bringing them upstairs to clutter up my cell. We're
about to start the canonical year. That's the strictest time of all
in the Novitiate. I can't even get letters, except on major
feasts."

When I came back from three o'clock Rosary, they were
dozing. Mother was leaning against Daddy's shoulder. I
remembered.

"Happy Anniversary!" I called as I crossed the lawn toward
them. "I almost forgot."

"So did I," Daddy said, rubbing his eyes.

They told the story every anniversary. Back in 1929 he'd showed up a day too soon, on August 26 instead of August 27. *"Poor Henry! You can imagine the teasing he had to take."*

All their fights about the checkbook and Harry Truman had not left scars. They looked ripe as honeymooners. Maybe bickering was a ritual of the married state, a kind of mindless prayer, like the Rosary.

"Would you like the grand tour?" I asked. "You've never seen the grounds."

Hoping to find a breeze, I led them down the shady walk that passed the community cemetery. "Death is a big deal here," I said, trying to sound enthusiastic. I described how on the day of death the community met the body in the front hall of the Motherhouse and said the fifteen mysteries around the coffin. The next morning, after a Solemn High Requiem Mass, everybody chanted the "Dies Irae" while processing to the cemetery for the burial.

"If a body meets a body," Daddy sang. He took Mother's arm and led her over to see the trillium under the pine trees on the right side of the cemetery gates.

It was much cooler down at the cemetery, but then the path wound uphill past the apple orchard and we were back in the sun. "Those apple trees need attention," Daddy said, examining a branch. He pointed at the newest and only modern building at Our Lady of the Woods. "What's that?"

"The Infirmary. The old nuns live there. I'm assigned to work in the Infirmary kitchen this year. I think I told you, the canonical year is mostly manual work and studying the vows."

"Why is it called a canonical year, Martha? Wait a minute. Is that a birdbath of Saint Francis?" She whipped out her

Brownie from her huge white pocketbook. "Stand in front of it, Martha, and don't block the statue."

I obeyed. "It's called a canonical year because it's Canon Law that says you have to spend a year of intense preparation before taking vows." She wasn't listening. She didn't care about Canon Law. She cared about getting me, the ugly birdbath, and the Infirmary all in the same frame.

As we passed the laundry building, through the window I saw the clock behind the big mangle. The bell for Vespers was not far off. I asked for news of Irene and Nony.

Nony's David had had a bad case of the mumps, though that could be a blessing in disguise. Now that Phil had been in Vietnam almost a year, Nony's youngest child thought that every soldier she saw on television was her father. Mother and Daddy planned to give Nony the piano when they retired to New Hampshire. Irene was carrying on. It was up to her to tell me the gory details. She and Steve were still going to their local parish priest for marriage counseling.

"I don't mean to be facetious," Daddy said. "But maybe you can tell us what in the hell does the clergy know about marriage?"

All of a sudden I remembered it was my day to put away the milk and cookies after Collation.

I thanked them for coming, kissed them good-bye fast, and invited them to Vespers.

"But there's so much I haven't told you—" Mother had tears in her eyes. "To come all this way . . . did I write you that Daddy's last cardiogram was perfect?"

Sweeping up the cooky crumbs in the Novitiate kitchen, I remembered Sister Cecilia, the principal of St. Francis of Assisi, telling off my first grade teacher. *"But my dear Sister, some things are much more important than the Horarium!"*

I couldn't see them at Vespers. As a Novice I had been assigned a new choir stall in the back of chapel. It was on the first tier of right choir, perpendicular to the raised platform that held Mother General's stall. Chanting the Office for the first time in the habit, right under her nose, made me self-conscious. I made mistakes, mispronouncing the Latin words, forgetting to incline at the Glorias. Big Mother is watching, I thought, as I kissed my scapular again and again. When you committed a fault in choir, you had to kiss your scapular.

In honor of our Reception there was Benediction after Vespers. We sang a hymn taken from Vespers for the Feast of the Immaculate Conception.

> *Tota pulchra est Maria*
> *et macula originalis*
> *non est in te.*
>
> *Tu gloria Jerusalem*
> *Tu laetitia Israel*
> *Tu honorificentia populi nostri. . . .*

The music of the hymn was ordinary, but the sound of the Latin words lifted me up. *Tu laetitia Israel!* I liked being back in chapel after a long visiting day in the sun. The chatter of the world was exhausting when you weren't used to it. The day had cooled off now. The habit wasn't itching or sticking to my skin. I looked across at left choir, at the Professed and Novices holding their hymnals and singing heartily. Sister Fides—until today, Dorothy Jackson from Zanesville—was pushing a stray wisp of hair back under her linen cap. I loved the Motherhouse right then. It felt quick with the energy of souls trying to live full of grace. *Ave Maria, gratia plena.* God is plenitude.

Mother General gave the signal to kneel as the parents filed out of chapel. I lifted my scapular carefully. We'd been warned that if you knelt on it it would wrinkle and might even tear at the shoulders. I caught a flash of my mother's raspberry silk near the side exit. I'd forgotten to compliment her on her new pearls, probably her anniversary present from Daddy. The next time I saw them would be Profession, when they'd drive out to see me take vows. "Is it wrong to think of Profession as your wedding day?" Mother had asked. I had never thought of it like that, of myself engaged to be married. But as I knelt in the Motherhouse chapel at the end of Reception day, I realized I had committed myself to something as serious just by putting on the habit. I had another year. To get ready, to give the place—the institution—a fair chance. To look at both sides. I would have to keep my wits about me. When the time came, I must be sure. Because once I made my vow, I'd keep it if it killed me.

Theology at Cherry Hill had surpassed even Philosophy for pure boredom. Through four required years of "Define the Church," "Define Tradition," "Define Transubstantiation," "Define your old man's backside," we took notes and looked forward to redemption by the bell. The only time Theology class came to life was in Senior year when we had a panel on birth control. I was assigned to present "The Protestant Position." After I'd finished reading my paper, Father Deedy said, "Eh, just a minute there Miss uh, Miss—did you get permission from your confessor to consult the sources you've quoted?" "No, Father," I said, bewildered. The class picked up its ears. Unused to our attention, Father Deedy blushed. "I assumed," he said nervously, "that a graduating Senior would know that you need official permission to read heresy. You all recognize, I trust, that the last paper we heard this morning contains heresy." His blush deepened as he then heard too many Seniors admit they liked the Protestant position better than *Casti connubi's*—Pius XII's encyclical on marriage was one of the required texts in Senior year Theology. "Define heresy!" he called as the bell delivered us from another abstraction and into the smoky cafeteria where we were lifted up by Suzy Daly's perfect imitation of poor Father Deedy.

The only text used in the Novices' Theology class at Our Lady of the Woods was the Bible. The teacher was a Scripture scholar, a young Dominican priest who defined nothing. In his strong passionate voice he read aloud passages from Isaiah, the Psalms, or the Gospel. Theology for him was the story of the God of history participating in the ongoing creation of the world He loved.

The long hours of manual work that made up a canonical Novice's day gave me time to turn over in my mind the earthy personality of a biblical—as opposed to an encyclical—religion. Each day I went through my tasks in the Infirmary's basement kitchen, struck not by the monotony of peeling and coring a bushel of apples but by a new preoccupation with the ordinary world—with history—as the setting for God's revelation of Himself. I was fascinated by biblical man—man not as he should be but as he is. Moses was a murderer but he didn't have to crawl on his belly. If we had talked to Sister Jane Agnes as directly as Abraham spoke up to Yahweh we would have lost our front teeth.

Sometimes I lost track of the day of the week and even of where I was I became so intent pondering the implications of the Exodus theme, of Isaiah's rage against the rich, of the contradiction between the idea of a loving, personal God and the historical facts of famines, concentration camps, and ugly marriages. After Mass one morning in October, as I peeled forty tangerines for the breakfasts of the old nuns who lived upstairs, I thought about the motif of energy in the Gospel. Christ was like an active verb. He helped people eat, drink, walk, see, wake up. Christianity was transitive, or should be. Its work should be about making the world transitive, slums becoming transformed into places where the phrase "the fullness of life" is not a mockery. At lunch time one day in November, while pitting forty canned plums, I had my first kind thoughts for St. Paul. (*"That woman hater,"* my mother had always snorted when his name was mentioned.) But the man who said, "The love of money is the root of all evil" had more to him than misogyny. I dolloped cottage cheese on forty lettuce leaves and recalled his words to Timothy quoted in that morning's Epistle:

> For God hath not given us the spirit of fear, but of power and
> of love, and of a sound mind.

I put the forty fruit salads on the trays and stacked the trays on the trolley. I started to clean up the mess of pits and unused limp brown lettuce leaves. Suddenly I thought of a topic for my Theology term paper, due at Christmas. Using selected biblical texts—or maybe just the story of Exodus—for supporting evidence, I'd show that the movement from fear to freedom was the very core—the heart—of religious experience. There was plenty of time to come up with a title.

Late one afternoon before Vespers, as I finished loading the forty supper trays onto the trolley, the Superior of the Infirmary kitchen told me to take the trolley up to the floors myself. "Are they short of help tonight! Mary Francis and Brigetta, both of them went to a wake in the city. And Francis Whosie—de Sales—she went to the . . . what's the fancy name for a foot doctor, Sister Elizabeth? I hear you're a fancy college girl."

When I pushed the trolley off the elevator onto the first three floors, the nun in charge took off the trays for that floor and delivered them to the rooms. But the Superior on Fourth, busily counting pills into tiny paper cups, told me to take the trays around to the rooms myself. Her hands were full.

I knocked on the first door. *"Benedicite!"* a voice shouted. I went in. A shrunken old nun looked blankly at me as I put her tray on the night table.

"Where's my Smuckers?" she shouted up at me. Then, as if scared by the sound of her own voice, she whined, "Celine *knows* I get Smuckers."

In the next room was a nun who made believe she was a fire engine when I put down her supper tray. Her siren went off so suddenly and it sounded so real that I laughed. The siren stopped. It looked straight ahead and said clearly, "Go to hell. Go to hell, snip."

In the rest of the rooms on Fourth I found one old lady after another, all in varying stages of senility. Some clutched at my sleeves, others smiled up at me from their wheelchairs or hospital beds like happy children. Seeing the sisters' emaciated bodies, I understood the trays filled with untouched fruit salads that always came back to the Infirmary kitchen from the Fourth floor.

The last tray on the trolley went to a room off by itself next to the elevator, where broom closets usually are. I didn't bother to knock. I opened the door quickly and entered a bedroom that was smaller than the others. There was a nun sitting in the dark. Unlike the other Sisters on Fourth, she was wearing the habit. In the light from the hallway she looked dead as stone. She didn't move when I set down her tray. I turned on her lamp and recognized her at once. It was Sister Cecilia, the principal of St. Francis Assisi, the gracious librarian and Latin teacher at Marymound. As I stood there staring, she looked up at me. She reached for my hand and held onto it very tight. She did not have the face of a happy child. She looked like living grief.

"Ah, Martha," she said. "I heard you were here."

Then, out in the hall the bell rang for Vespers.

That night during Recreation I mentioned having come upon Sister Cecilia to the Novice Mistress.

"What a marvelous Latin teacher she was," I said, looking for information.

"Indeed she was, Sister, indeed, she was. It was a terrible shock to all of us when Sister aged so quickly."

"Oh, then she's not really sick."

"On the contrary, Sister Elizabeth. Senility is a very serious sickness because we know so little about it."

She ended the conversation by motioning me toward the piano. The novices sang and I played the accompaniment to "Climb Every Mountain," always Number One in the Novitiate's "Make Believe Ballroom." I glanced up at the faces around the piano bleating out *The Sound of Music* mush. Sister Cecilia's mind is as sound as any fool's in this room, I thought.

Our Novice Mistress was a strange bird. Every day after noon dinner, Sister Alexandrine mounted the platform in the Novitiate classroom, opened her arms up toward the crucifix and called: *"Pour forth we beseech Thee, O Lord, Thy grace into our hearts . . ."* Then for sixty minutes she gave us "instructions," tossing down home truths on the vows of poverty, chastity, and obedience. "Answer the sound of the bell as if it were the voice of Almighty God Himself and you will come to *love* your vow of obedience." Occasionally she rose to eloquent heights and then the novices looked up at her full handsome figure in adoration. "The laity is important, my little sisters, as arms and legs are to any creature; but we religious are the *heart* of the church, without which the Mystical Body of Christ Our Lord would be cold indeed!" Mostly, she pecked away at our fears with stories about nuns who left the convent and either married unhappily or never conceived, or, what was most common, never found a husband in the first place. "Nobody wants an ex-nun," she warned, narrowing her pretty blue eyes. "Poor Sister Michael Ann—Mary Rooney in the world—she left us and then changed her mind and wanted to come back, but Mother General wouldn't take her. She still writes to me, a very unhappy, single woman to this day."

Sister Alexandrine called us her chicks. Usually she reminded me of nothing more complicated than a mother hen as she hugged a homesick novice to her full breast or scolded someone for sloppy housework. "The Sister who dusted the Recreation Room this morning has a lot to learn about seeking perfection. Sister Agnes Marie, I could have written my name in the dust you left on the sewing table. What does 'Be ye perfect' mean to you, Sister? Stand up when you're spoken to, Sister!"

Sometimes, though, the Mistress of Novices flew a mutinous course, raising her eyebrows in dismay as Mother General, from the head table in the Refectory, announced yet another departure from tradition. Sometimes, too, Sister Alexandrine seemed devious. She called me into her office once to say she'd gotten a report from Mother General that I was reading poetry during Meditation.

"I think that's a beautiful way to use your Meditation, Sister Elizabeth, but I wouldn't say that to Mother General—she's a Midwesterner and you must have noticed these Midwesterners have no imagination. Aren't they a dull breed, Sister?"

She grabbed my hand as if we were conspirators.

She was a New Yorker too, from "Washington Heights, when it was still Irish territory."

At two o'clock one raw gray Friday, the Chant Mistress began the Postulants' and Novices' weekly choir practice for Sunday's High Mass. The entire community was supposed to chant the Proper. The Schola, a group of eight novices who could best carry a tune, was supposed to be able to lead the community from *clivis* to *climacus* to the last Amen. On the Steinway in the music room, Sister Jeremy, our Chant Mistress, banged the notes of the Introit for the Last Sunday After Pentecost. Then she sang the first phrase *a cappella*. *"Dicit Dominus Ego cogito cogitationes pacis . . ."* "Okay, Schola, take it—*Dicit . . ."* The Schola began chanting and faded out halfway through *Dominus.* Only Sister Fides chanted on, doggedly out of tune.

"Is that ever sick!" Sister Jeremy shouted. "You know, Schola, after a year of chant class you should be able to tell a simple *clivis* from a *porrectus flexus."*

As the First Chantress intoned the *Dicit Dominus* again, a Professed Sister opened the door of the music room. She walked briskly over to the piano, whispered to Sister Jeremy, and left.

"Wow!" Sister Jeremy said. "He's been shot! Kennedy . . . Take it again, Schola, this time the whole Introit without stopping."

We were practicing the Offertory chant when the Professed Sister returned. She whispered again to Sister Jeremy. Sister Jeremy looked vaguely over the top of the grand piano. "Well, what do you know?" she said in a casual voice. "He's dead."

She continued the choir practice, ignoring the sniffling of a few Novices. At three o'clock she stood up. She was six feet, five inches tall. When she was in the world, she'd told us, she'd played a mean game of ice hockey. "That'll have to do till warm-up Sunday morning," she said. "You know, Schola, Mother General was visibly upset after last Sunday's High Mass. You blew the Offertory . . . Can you believe they got him? Personally, I could never stand him."

Upstairs in the Novitiate it was time for afternoon Collation. The Novice Mistress turned on the television and we took the news from Dallas along with our milk and cookies. The Novice Mistress was upset and so the Novices acted very solemn. When Sister Alexandrine left the Recreation Room, Sister Mary Jane said this was a good time to discuss final plans for the entertainment at Sister Alexandrine's birthday party on Saturday night. "She won't want the party now," I said. But they went ahead and rehearsed their little skit just in case. Mother General had been invited. If the entertainment was not well rehearsed, Sister Alexandrine would be disgraced on her birthday by her own baby chicks.

Friday night we watched the body being taken off the plane at Andrew's Air Force Base. I had often lost patience since Kennedy's election. On civil rights he's gutless, I'd insisted to my mother, who defended any Democrat on principle. But the day he died I remembered his energy. Kennedy made words like "work" and "future" seem full of possibility. I had unconsciously made his New Frontier the context for the evolving world Teilhard de Chardin evoked in *The Divine Milieu*. Now, as I watched the old news clips of Kennedy in Berlin, in Wexford, at the Dallas airport that morning, I felt the idea of possibility losing ground. In the glare from the television I saw the Novices passing around boxes of Kleenex and I heard them blowing their noses and laughing through their tears apologetically.

"Oh, Sister, isn't this awful?"

"I know, Sister, I just can't help it. I haven't cried like this since our last visiting day."

"Did you see Sister Mary Michael at supper? Her eyes were like *slits!*"

"Sister Mary Jane, you look *aw*ful!"

"I know, Sister. I'm really surprised at myself. I didn't even know anything about him. I was only in my Junior year in high school when he ran for the Presidency."

The Novice Mistress did not cancel her birthday party on Saturday night. On Sunday morning she was vindicated.

The celebrant of the High Mass was George Egan, the altar boy from St. Francis Assisi who had made Irene, Nony, and me the targets of his snowball blitz after the Christmas-week blizzard of 1947. Newly ordained in Rome, he'd come to the Motherhouse to visit his sister and to personally thank the community that had first nurtured his vocation.

His sermon was about triumph, his own, first of all. "To have heard the call of God to His priesthood and to have had the grace to answer His call, this I count as a great personal victory."

Then he spoke of the Vatican Council as signifying the triumph of the Holy Spirit over the spirit of fear that for too long had made Holy Mother Church about as vigorous as an old lady counting her teaspoons.

I didn't care for the image. I put my hands under my scapular and played "Here's the church and here's the steeple" with my fingers. I felt the eyes of Mother General on me as I wiggled them at the line "Open it up and see all the people."

Up in the pulpit George Egan was saying that the assassination of the President offered the Christian the opportunity to make faith triumph over the world. "The nation weeps," he said, "because it does not believe in Christ's Resurrection. Christ has triumphed over death, and so, therefore, have we, His followers. I think we may safely assume that President Kennedy, as a baptized Catholic who frequented the sacraments, is now in Purgatory. And with our prayers, he will soon share in Christ's glorious Resurrection. Our tears for him, therefore, betray a lack of faith in the central Christian mystery. For, my dear Sisters of Our Lady of the Woods, for the Christian"—like Kennedy used to do, he jabbed at the air with his index finger—"for the Christian, there is no such thing as a tragedy. I repeat: for the Christian, there can be no tragedy. For us, there is only triumph."

I stared across choir at a misericord on an empty stall. After Mass we watched Jack Ruby shoot Oswald, and then the stunned-looking widow lead her daughter forward to kiss the casket of the dead husband and father. The Novitiate was chirpy and smiling all that Sunday and also on Monday. For, as Father Egan had expressed it so beautifully, we Christian people shouldn't carry on like a bunch of pagans, weeping and wailing as if there's no tomorrow.

I kept my pagan tears hidden behind the bathroom door. On Monday, the day of the funeral and burial, I was assigned to deliver the dinner trays to Infirmary Fourth. As I wheeled the trolley off the elevator, I saw a cluster of wheelchairs around a tiny television at the end of the corridor. The senile old nuns were watching the funeral procession down Pennsylvania Avenue. I stood behind them and watched their broken-hearted faces watching the end of Kennedy. Sister Cecilia held her head in her hands, as if she could not bear to look too closely at this link in a great chain of waste.

"May his soul and all the souls of the faithful departed rest in peace," she said quietly as the procession entered Arlington cemetery.

From the wheelchairs came a chorus of Amens.

"Get out of here with those damn fruit salads," Sister Callista ordered me. "Can't you see that poor young man is *dead?"*

Then we began the liturgical season of Advent, the time to prepare for the coming of the Redeemer in grace and in His final glory. The Schola practiced every day. Besides the Propers for the three Masses of Christmas, we had to learn the "O Antiphons" that were sung at Mass, starting on December 17. The "O" or "Great" antiphons were seven: "O Sapientia" (O Wisdom, . . . Come and teach us the way of prudence); "O Adonai" (O Adonai, Come and with an outstretched arm redeem us); "O Radix Jesse" (O Root of Jesse, Come to deliver us and tarry not); "O Clavis David" (O Key of David, Come and bring forth from his prison-house, the captive that sitteth in darkness and in the shadow of death); "O Oriens" (O Dawn of the East, Come and enlighten them that sit in darkness and in the shadow of death); "O Rex Gentium" (O

King of the Gentiles, Come and deliver man whom Thou didst form out of the dust of the earth); "O Emmanuel" (O Emmanuel, Come to save us).

The Advent liturgy had a tone of confidence and expectation. *Take courage and fear not,* read Isaiah, *for behold He Himself will come to save us.* Our Theology term papers were due the last class before Christmas. My topic—religious experience in the Bible as a going out from fear and coming into a spirit of freedom—was of the season.

As I went about my jobs in the Infirmary kitchen, I enjoyed thinking about the parts of the paper that would deal with the spirit of freedom. The Old and New Testaments abounded with stories of people who, one way or another, had found their own voices—Abraham, Moses, Osee, Mary, David. You could never cover them all in the same paper. Thinking about the free spirits in the Bible reminded me of the ones I'd known personally—Sister Miriam when she talked about literature, Robert Emmet singing, Nony in the Greyhound bus station in Richmond, Virginia.

As I went about the Novitiate, I did not enjoy noticing the signs of fear. The Novices were afraid of the Novice Mistress. Some of them, when they saw her coming, quickly put on their blue and white checked aprons, to make her think they were virtuously going about their Father's business, cleanliness being next to godliness. In the dormitory, afraid of Sister Alexandrine's wrath, we cleaned our cells to perfection; in the laundry, afraid to be caught slacking on the job, we folded and pressed all things perfectly; in chapel we contemplated perfection with our eyes wide open, afraid to be thought sleeping; in the Refectory we ate cautiously, afraid we'd have to perform the public penance attached to certain "faults," such as dropping a fork at table.

The Chant Mistress was afraid of Mother General. "We have to do the 'Rorate Coeli' perfectly, Schola. It's Mother General's favorite."

Mother General kowtowed to the Bishop. When Bishop Stubbs came to the Woods the First Sunday of Advent to announce a drive for a ten-million-dollar building fund, Mother General immediately—and nervously—pledged that our community would do its part. Through the Novice Mistress she passed on orders to the Novitiate to turn out as many hand-made aprons as humanly possible in time to be sold at the Bishop's Christmas Bazaar.

The Novice Mistress was afraid of being raped. One Sunday morning I was sweeping the hall outside her office. Suddenly she opened her door and took me by the arm. "If you ever leave here, Sister Elizabeth," she said, "whatever you do, do not get married. How would you like to have to share your bed with someone who comes home in the middle of the night drunk and smelly? You must, you know." Her private view of marriage had far more feeling than her classroom explanation of the vow of chastity. Both, I assumed, as I stood leaning on my broom handle, derived from a childhood of listening to a drunken father return at midnight from the local Blarney Stone to torture her mother on the other side of little Sister Alexandrine's bedroom wall.

I decided to change the topic of my theology paper. I did not have enough experience to write about freedom, whether in the Bible or in the real world. And I did not understand fear, though I had often felt it tugging at me—*back off, hurry up, lay low, why bother, shut up, not now!* Its signals were never the same, but it always left the same shrinking feeling.

And then one lucky morning, the Novice Mistress posted a notice on the Novitiate bulletin board.

> God is with you, my dear Novices. Your Theology instructor, Father Grimes, has been called home indefinitely. Your term paper is, therefore, cancelled! As you enter the final weeks of Advent, let us continue to prepare our hearts for the Christ Child. Let us give thanks for one another. Let us spend ALL OUR EXTRA TIME ON THE APRONS FOR THE BISHOP'S BA-ZAAR!!! You may speak while you sew. Remember the words from the Psalm which we read in this morning's Gradual—"My mouth shall speak the praise of the Lord."

We sewed after breakfast. We sewed in the afternoons when we usually had Theology and our daily class on the vows. Every night after Complin we sewed till the gong for Profound Silence.

Sister Pascal confided her love of the smell of airplane glue. Sister Mary Jane said her father hadn't once spoken to her since the night she announced she wanted to enter the convent. Sister Mary Norbert from Louisville said that Southerners should not be condemned—"so many Negroes in a place made the situation very difficult, *so* difficult, Sisters, you can't know!"

Sister Dolores and I argued about the habit. I said it was impractical. The twelve hours the community spent in the laundry every Saturday should be spent taking courses, reading about whatever our work was. Sister Dolores said if we wore regular street clothes we'd have to spend even more time keeping them up to date than we did in the laundry. "Anyway we should wear special clothes because we *are* special. As Sister Alexandrine expressed it so beautifully, we're the heart of the church."

I proposed to the Novice Mistress that the thrice daily sewing marathons might be a good time to learn Spanish. We could set up the tape recorder in a separate room for those who were interested. When the Sisters from the Peru mission had visited the Motherhouse the summer before, they'd left tapes of their introductory Spanish course with the Novice Mistress. "So you future missionaries can learn to parlez-vous in español," she'd told us at the time.

"Not that all of us are going to volunteer for the Peru mission," I said. "But Spanish would be useful to any teacher in New York these days. Or in any big city." She was the one who lamented how New York had changed every time she mentioned the place.

Sister Alexandrine bit, but not greedily. "All right, Sister, you have my permission. I'll post a notice for your Sister Novices. After Complin, there will be Spanish. Be careful, Sister Elizabeth, that you do not get carried away by the spirit of the times. As hard as I try to keep the world out of the Novitiate, it gets through, it gets through, Sister. This current emphasis we have nowadays on action is not good. It's not good, Sister. This idea that everything must be relevant . . . Poor Sister John Vianney was telling me just this afternoon that she is required to study something called 'the New Grammar' as part of her Master's program at Ohio State. Her professor says the Old Grammar is not relevant to much of today's world. I tell you, Sister Elizabeth, this world is too much with us. It's not good."

Besides myself, three Novices out of twenty-six showed up

the first night of Spanish class, two, the second. Soon it was down to Sister Dolores and me practicing our duet to the signals of the tape recorder.

"Buenos días, niños, ¿Cómo están? Me llamo Hermana Dolores."

"Buenos días, niños. ¿Cómo están? Me llamo Hermana Elizabeth."

We couldn't hear the tape very well. It was poorly made and the sounds of laughing and gabbling from the Recreation Room drowned it out in many spots.

One night the Novice Mistress opened the door and smiled into the large almost empty classroom. Sister Dolores and I stood up.

"Poor Sister Elizabeth," she said. "That's enough español for one night. Come and have some cake. It's Sister Mary Sean's birthday, you know."

It took a few minutes to rewind the tape and pack up the tape recorder, close the windows, adjust the blinds. I moved slowly. I felt as if I had already gorged myself on the fake butter cream of another birthday cake.

"No one in this place is serious about work."

"I think that's rash judging, Sister Elizabeth, I really do. Making aprons and, I'd say, giving a birthday party is work— it's all part of our community life," Sister Dolores said.

From the Common Room came the sound of "Climb Every Mountain" *a cappella.*

"Adiós, amigos," I said, flipping off the overhead light. "My name is Martha Girlinghausen." *Whatta lotta sheet.*

We sang three Masses on Christmas, at midnight, at dawn, and at midday. The beauty of the liturgy made the feast as full of joy as it had been in childhood. "Sing ye to the Lord a new canticle," we sang. "Because He hath done wonderful things." All the texts—Isaiah, Daniel, the Psalms, Luke, Paul —they said that we believed that all the peoples of the world had been set free. We'd been set free from fear. This birth we celebrated had given the world a new start. We could choose to love one another, to build the earth for one another. "Fear not," the angel told the cringing shepherds.

But from my stall I watched the Novice Mistress, high in left choir, even on Christmas eyeing her Novices furtively, looking for sleepyheads during Meditation. And before Mass at dawn, the Chant Mistress kicked Sister Fides out of the Schola. Mother General had complained that her voice had been raspy during the midnight service. After that happened the Schola picked up the chants from the First and Second Chantresses very timidly. The cringing shepherds had multiplied and filled the earth. During the sermon I remembered it was sixteen years to the hour since Daddy's Christmas heart attack.

Christmas night the Novices went carolling through the Infirmary. Most of the senile nuns on Fourth were asleep. A few were watching television. A small tree had been set up on top of it. I looked at the blinking colored lights and remembered what Bold Robert Emmet had said one Christmas night at our house in Flushing. The Christmas tree reminded him of a city—all the different colors and objects on it, its depths and hidden parts—its possibilities.

As we carolled past Sister Cecilia's room, I stopped and knocked on her door. Inside, she explained why she was living on Infirmary Fourth. Sister Cecilia had had a slight stroke after Mother General had assigned her to teach typing at a high school in Zanesville. "There was no explanation, you see. I'd spent my life in the Classics and doing library work and administration. Then out of nowhere came the order to teach typing. I may have had a stroke but I didn't lose my mind. But here I sit. Once a week a young man from Ohio State comes in here, a Ph.D. in Psychology, to find out why I'm not happy and report back to Mother General." She smiled up at me from her wheelchair. "Isn't that the limit?"

For the New Year, Mother General resolved to put Our Lady of the Woods in touch with the modern world: instead of the Martyrology which was usually read aloud in the Refectory on Saturday nights we were to hear selected readings from *Time* magazine. Mother General also resolved that the entire community—at the Woods, on the missions, even the Canonical Novices—should watch Walter Cronkite when their schedules permitted.

I resolved to hang on. You don't give up on the heart of the church overnight.

Every evening of the New Year, then, in accordance with Mother General's resolution, the Novice Mistress entrusted to me the responsibility of turning on the television after dinner and turning it off when the bell rang for Complin. The Novices who were not assigned to tidy the Refectory gathered obediently in the vicinity of the "Evening News" program. Some passed the time playing ping-pong on the new table given by Sister Rita's parents. Others spent the half hour exchanging the day's news from around the Motherhouse while making door prizes for the diocesan spring card party, another benefit for the Bishop's building fund. Walter Cronkite had nothing to say about the way it was in March, April, or May of 1964 that could summon that audience to attention. Most of it left him early to spend a few quiet minutes before Complin visiting the Blessed Sacrament and putting the modern world in its place—*sub specie aeternitatis,* where there was only Christian triumph.

But one hot night in June, Cronkite had a story of loss that neither the sport around the ping-pong table nor the transcendent sound of Compline could overpower. Three young men, civil rights' workers, had disappeared on a Sunday night in Mississippi. Twenty-four hours later they were still missing. After Compline, when Mother General gave the signal to kneel for silent prayer, I remembered their names—James Chaney, Michael Schwerner, and Andrew Goodman.

The search for their bodies became the lead story on the "Evening News." As I listened to reports about the KKK and imagined what it would do to one Negro and two Jews caught working to register Negroes to vote, I knew the three young men had been murdered. Even Cronkite, whose face and tone of voice usually made the ways of the world seem benign, reported the ongoing search as if it were an inexorable advance into darkness. I knew they were dead. But every night I went to Compline and beseeched the Lord of Justice and Mercy to bring them back alive.

The summer dragged on. Though hope was exhausted, I still switched on the news and waited for Cronkite to announce there had been a miracle—Chaney, Goodman, and

Schwerner had been found hiding out on a mountain in Tennessee, hungry but alive. I prayed for it obsessively. In my mind they became saints. *Greater love than this no man hath, that he lay down his life for his friends.* I thought most about Andrew Goodman. He was from Queens. He had hardly had time to realize what he was getting into. A month before he had heard a speech about the Civil Rights Movement in the Queens College auditorium and decided out of nowhere to go south. His father looked so decent on television.

"Hey, Sister Elizabeth, would you turn that TV down? It's distracting Sister Fides from her game. Four-three, Fides, Sister Rita's favor!"

No one was playing ping-pong the August night Cronkite announced their bodies had been found. The Novices were outside setting up the gazebo for a pizza party to be held that night during Recreation. I watched the pictures of the muddy hole in which they had been buried, of the Navy accomplishing their resurrection. I wept and wept. There had been no miracle.

At the close of Compline, before the pizza party, Mother General stood up in her choir stall:

"Sisters, I wish to request the prayers of the community for a very special intention, one that I know is very close to the heart of every sister at Our Lady of the Woods—please pray for the continued success of the Bishop's building fund."

In a sacramental universe even tooth decay can give grace. One of my impacted wisdom teeth had been neglected too long. The day after the three bodies were found in Mississippi, the Novice Mistress gave me permission to join a station wagon load of Professed that was going into Columbus to a dentist.

It was the first time I'd been outside the iron gates of Our Lady of the Woods in more than a year. Even the suburbs we had to pass through delighted me. Downtown, though we were supposed to keep the "guard on the eyes," I walked along behind the Professed taking in the street life. The Professed reminded me of Rosie O'Grady the time we'd walked into the city from Flushing—they looked neither left nor right. In the car they'd traded gossip about the parents of this student, the boldness of that one, was it true that Mother General was bringing the Sisters home from the Peru mission? In the dentist's office they read their Office; I stared at the people who were staring at me.

On the way back to the Motherhouse we went through the Negro section of Columbus—I don't know if by accident or to save time or what. Then the Professed woke up. Off came the "guard on the eyes." From my seat in the back of the station wagon I heard a few clichés about urban blight, the plight of white homeowners, the deterioration of property values. A few Professed kept quiet, I couldn't tell for what reason—did they agree, disagree, not care? Was their Novacaine wearing off and their fillings and holes or new dentures driving them crazy?

The station wagon slowed and pulled through the gates at the bottom of the long driveway leading up to the Motherhouse. Inside I had that shrinking feeling, the sign of the presence of fear. I'd kept quiet, too. I was filled with self-disgust. But that in itself was a kind of grace—I was nobody to cast stones.

"Well, I must say you shock me, Sister Elizabeth. I thought you were happy." The Novice Mistress stood with her back against her closed office door.

"I am. I have been."

"You could have a great future with us, you know. You could have been President of our college."

She reminded me of the interviewer at the Peace Corps. Both observed a similar commandment: Thou shalt not commit vocational suicide.

She sat down behind her desk. "Have you considered staying and trying to change the community from within? Every institution has its imperfections."

I had never told the truth to one of them. I spoke quickly before I lost my nerve.

"I think the community is hopeless."

"Don't you think the Council will help to change communities such as ours?"

"I think the structure of the whole church is hopeless."

Sister Alexandrine put her head in her hands and sighed, as if exhausted. "This may shock you," she said. "But I agree with you—I have often thought along similar lines. But I can't leave. Where would I go at my age? Nobody wants an ex-nun."

I told her I didn't know where I was going either, had no plans, but that was fatuous of me. I was twenty-one. She was afraid and old. She'd repeated her propaganda about ex-nuns so often (to reassure herself?) that it had paralyzed her.

Then her face tightened and she stood up abruptly. "I'll arrange your parting interview with Mother General." She held her office door wide open for me. "And now, what you do, do quickly, Judas."

The tyrant has a mind like a ghetto, closed and suspicious.

"I hear you think the structure of the church is hopeless." Mother General's eyes were hard. "That makes you a heretic."

I laughed out loud.

"What *is* your definition of the church, may I ask?" She spoke calmly.

Sitting there, I realized that all of a sudden I didn't care what it was. I'd looked at the heart; there was no more mystery.

"Well, I don't know," I said. "Christ came to save the world. Maybe the church is the world."

She pounced triumphantly. *"That* was defined as heresy when Duns Scotus said it in the thirteenth century." She leaned toward me across her desk. It was the first time she'd moved her body.

"May I ask a question?" I said.

Mother General nodded.

"Who is Andrew Goodman?"

There was silence. Then, simultaneously, her eyes narrowed, her brows knitted, and her lips became pursed. She stared at me intently, as if she were on the verge of insight.

"You're not for us—you're the kind who is concerned with becoming rather than being. Religious life is about being."

I felt like asking her what she was doing on the throne of an active order instead of a cloistered one. But instead I asked why she had *Time* magazine read aloud in the Refectory.

"We're under siege," she said. "We at the heart of the church, especially. It's wise policy to read up on the enemy's strategy."

Her *aggiornamento* was like the punch they ladled out at Cherry Hill on public occasions—it was all cherry syrup with not enough booze to fill a midget's thimble. "Mother General is more and more on the side of aggiornamento," Sister Miriam had written. I wondered what she'd do when she found out Mother General was a fake.

"I think I know why you're really leaving us," she said as I stood up. She sounded coy. "Is there someone waiting for you? I always thought you were the marrying kind—"

I never found out if by that she meant I'd always reminded her of a whore. Did she think I'd been having the hots right under her nose in right choir? I think it meant only that she had an either/or plate in her head—a woman either joins a convent or marries a man. There are no other ways of being and/or becoming.

I packed my bag and called Greyhound. I wanted a long ride, not a short plane trip. The next morning the Novice Mistress gave me back my hundred-dollar dowry, and I took off.

In the Columbus bus terminal I started reading my mail. The Novice Mistress had left it on top of my suitcase, opened and with a note attached.

I withheld these letters when the holiday mail was distributed on Christmas and Easter. They are nothing for a Canonical

Novice. They come from the *world* you're returning to, God help you.

Within a card from an old good-time-Charlie friend were a few photographs of couples on the shore of Lake Shoshone out West and one of me and him on top of the Little Bighorn. Charlie wrote "Merry Christmas! When I heard what you'd done with yourself, I could not believe it. I guess I'll never understand women. Good luck."

Then there was a card signed "Love, Bold Robert Emmet." He'd written a short tame message. I couldn't imagine why the Novice Mistress had withheld so noncommittal a greeting.

Her objections to the next two letters I understood. The letter from Nina Iondola began:

My dearest Martha,

I hope to come to the Woods for your Profession of vows next summer, but before that I want to tell you so many things that fill my mind and heart. How I long to see you in person. But let me begin at the beginning. It will probably surprise you, my dear friend, to hear that I have decided not to enter the Carmelites after all. Isn't it strange that you, who always blasphemed so and called *me* a religious maniac, should be the one to enter religious life and not I? To put it briefly, my philosophical arguments with the Council of Admissions at the Carmelite Monastery finally became irreconcilable. They concerned the meaning of transcendence and of contemplation, to name just two. Also, I have had many difficult responsibilities at home during this past year. My sister had a nervous breakdown at the end of the school year. The Prefect of Discipline at Mercy High School, where she was a Sophomore, accused her of writing a note during Latin class that had the word "cunt" in it. When they tried to expel her, my father, who is not well, threatened

to bring a lawsuit against the community, but then he became
so ill he had to be hospitalized. My sister and he have never had
a very good relationship and Janet is very sensitive. All the
trouble at school must have been affecting her more than any
of us realized. Over the summer she just went to pieces. It is
very tragic at home—my mother's heart is broken and my
father is too sick himself to help her. Please, Martha, keep us
all in your prayers.

Despite all of this pain, I am so happy! I am living with the
man I love in a large walk-up near the Queensboro Bridge
(Manhattan side). Fernando is from Spain. We met in a graduate seminar on the Cambridge Platonists last summer at Yale.
Fernando is waiting for his papers to come from Rome. He has
asked to be released from his vows and to leave the priesthood.

I hope you haven't changed too much, dear Martha. I long
to see you and have you meet Fernando. I took him to our spot
in High Bridge Park, but he prefers the view of the Fifty-ninth
Street Bridge from our sanctuary on the East River.

All my love always,
Nina

I opened Nony's letter as the bus pulled out of the Columbus
terminal.

. . . I know how much we both worry about her, so after much
consideration I've decided you should know that Irene has
decided to get a divorce. I realize that coming from this distance this news may upset you. Believe me, Martha, her spirit
is strong, due, I'm sure, to your constant prayers for her. She
feels the children are suffering badly and the priest–marriage
counselor has been wasting her time. He has sided with Steve
all along, who quotes St. Thomas on the inferiority of women
and the indissolubility of marriage by turns.

The children and I are busy with Easter—dyed 15 dozen
eggs for the Children's Shelter in D.C. Phil comes home from

his tour in Vietnam next fall. In the meantime I must convince
David that his father is not dead. David never left the TV set
when JFK died and sometime over that long unreal weekend
he got the notion that his daddy had died too and is now in
heaven with Kennedy and "Macaroni" (Caroline's pony that
he no longer sees on the White House lawn when we drive
past). My special intention right now (make it yours, too) is that
Phil will decide to resign his commission. That's about as likely
as your showing up in the Easter Parade—not too many West
Pointers throw in the sponge. Ordinarily, I don't like to think
along such hard lines, but, honestly, Martha, I am less and less
impressed with Army life. . . .

I sat back and gazed out the window. The farms in the
distance and the cornfields under random clouds reminded me
of Bruegel's *The Harvest.* Then my seat mate opened his newspaper and brought me back inside the bus. Every time he
turned the page of his *Columbus Dispatch* he rubbed the back
of his hand across my breasts. The whole time I went up and
down the aisle looking for a different seat the bus driver
yelled, "Sit down, lady, I'm pulling over and not moving this
bus until you sit down."

I found an empty seat, but at Pittsburgh I got off the Colum-
bus–New York bus. I bought a new ticket for Washington,
D.C. I'd stop off at Nony's before heading home. I'd looked
forward all night long to seeing the city towering over the
Hudson, to being in New York on my own at last. But now,
I wanted to see Nony again.